Discourses of the Prophet
JOSEPH
SMITH

THE PROPHET JOSEPH SMITH

Discourses of the Prophet

JOSEPH SMITH

COMPILED AND ARRANGED
By
ALMA P. BURTON

First Edition
1956

Published by
DESERET BOOK COMPANY
Salt Lake City, Utah

Printed By
Deseret News Press
In the United States of America

Foreword

The statements of doctrine and items of procedure in Church government, as taught by the Prophet Joseph Smith, have been published, in whole or in part, by others and by the Church of Jesus Christ of Latter-day Saints.

Elder Franklin D. Richards, an apostle of the Church and Church Historian for many years, and Elder James A. Little published a book entitled *A Compendium of the Doctrines of the Gospel*. One chapter in this book is devoted to "Gems from the History of Joseph Smith." The statements used were taken from the manuscript history of the Church and other records of the Prophet Joseph Smith.

The manuscript history was published, beginning in 1902, as the *History of the Church* by Joseph Smith. This work was prepared for publication by the Church Historian and his assistants and has been referred to, over a period of many years, as the *Documentary History of the Church*.

A publication of doctrinal items taught by the Prophet Joseph Smith was prepared and published by Elder Edwin F. Parry, under the title *Joseph Smith's Teachings*.

Elder Joseph Fielding Smith, President of the Quorum of the Twelve Apostles and Historian of the Church, has published the doctrinal statements from the *History of the Church* and other statements by the Prophet. These publications are entitled *Teachings of the Prophet Joseph Smith* and *Church History and Modern Revelation*, the latter is a two-volume work. These books are in constant use.

The compiler of this book has felt for many years that it would be of service to the members of the Church, as well as others, if the teachings of our beloved Prophet Joseph Smith were arranged and classified according to subject matter. For this reason this book has been arranged, compiled, and published. Doctrines from the Book of Mormon, the Doctrine and Covenants, and the Pearl of Great Price have not been included.

Most of the material for this book has been taken from the *History of the Church* by Joseph Smith. Excerpts from such important sermons as the King Follett discourse, have been classified into different subject areas in this publication; however, the reader may see the statement in context by referring to the *History of the Church* as indicated by the volume and page accompanying the reference *D.H.C.* Other references are given in full at the conclusion of each quotation. For these reasons a bibliography has been omitted.

It is the hope of the compiler that this book will assist all who read it better to understand the Prophet Joseph Smith and the doctrines and practices established in the Church in this the Dispensation of the Fulness of Times.

—ALMA P. BURTON

Contents

Chapter One

God and Man

The Character of God

. . . It is the first principle of the gospel to know for a certainty the character of God, and to know that we may converse with him as one man converses with another, and that he was once a man like us; yea, that God himself, the Father of us all, dwelt on an earth, the same as Jesus Christ himself did; and I will show it from the Bible. (*D.H.C.* VI, 305)

Jehovah Contemplated All Things

The great Jehovah contemplated the whole of the events connected with the earth, pertaining to the plan of salvation before it rolled into existence, or ever "the morning stars sang together" for joy; the past, the present, and the future were and are, with him, one eternal "now"; he knew of the fall of Adam, the iniquities of the antediluvians, of the depth of iniquity that would be connected with the human family, their weakness and strength, their power and glory, apostasies, their crimes, their righteousness and iniquity; he comprehended the fall of man, and his redemption; he knew the plan of salvation and pointed it out; he was acquainted with the situation of all nations and with their destiny; he ordered all things according to the council of his own will; he knows the situation of both the living and the dead, and has made ample provision for their redemption, according to their several circumstances, and the laws of the kingdom of God, whether in this world, or in the world to come. (*D.H.C.* IV, 597)

Relationship of Man to God

The first principles of man are self-existent with God. God himself, finding he was in the midst of spirits and glory, because he was more intelligent, saw proper to institute laws whereby the rest could have a privilege to advance like himself. The relationship we have with God places us in a situation to advance in knowledge. He has power to institute laws to instruct the weaker intelligences, that they may be exalted with himself, so that they might have one glory upon another, and all that knowledge, power, glory, and intelligence, which is requisite in order to save them in the world of spirits. . . .

I want to talk more of the relation of man to God. I will open your eyes in relation to the dead. All things whatsoever God in his infinite wisdom has seen fit and proper to reveal to us, while we are dwelling in mortality, in regard to our mortal bodies, are revealed to us in the abstract, and independent of affinity of this mortal tabernacle, but are revealed to our spirits precisely as though we had no bodies at all; and those revelations which will save our spirits will save our bodies. God reveals them to us in view of no eternal dissolution of the body, or tabernacle. Hence the responsibility, the awful responsibility, that rests upon us in relation to our dead; for all the spirits who have not obeyed the Gospel in the flesh must either obey it in the spirit or be damned. Solemn thought!—dreadful thought! Is there nothing to be done?—no preparation—no salvation for our fathers and friends who have died without having had the opportunity to obey the decrees of the Son of Man? Would to God that I had forty days and nights in which to tell you all! (*D.H.C.* VI, 312-313)

Adam's Relationship as Head of the Human Race

Daniel in his seventh chapter speaks of the Ancient of Days; he means the oldest man, our Father Adam,

Michael, he will call his children together and hold a council with them to prepare them for the coming of the Son of Man. He (Adam) is the father of the human family, and presides over the spirits of all men, and all that have had the keys must stand before him in this grand council. This may take place before some of us leave this stage of action. The Son of Man stands before him, and there is given him glory and dominion. Adam delivers up his stewardship to Christ, that which was delivered to him as holding the keys of the universe, but retains his standing as head of the human family. (*D.H.C.* III, 386-387)

Foreordination

. . . Every man who has a calling to minister to the inhabitants of the world was ordained to that very purpose in the grand council of heaven before this world was. I suppose that I was ordained to this very office in that grand council. It is the testimony that I want that I am God's servant, and this people his people. (*D.H.C.* VI, 364)

Why Adam Blessed His Posterity

I saw Adam in the valley of Adam-ondi-Ahman. He called together his children and blessed them with a patriarchal blessing. The Lord appeared in their midst, and he (Adam) blessed them all, and foretold what should befall them to the latest generation.

This is why Adam blessed his posterity; he wanted to bring them into the presence of God. They looked for a city, etc., ["whose builder and maker is God."—Heb. xi:10]. Moses sought to bring the children of Israel into the presence of God, through the power of the priesthood, but he could not. In the first ages of the world they tried to establish the same thing; and there were Eliases raised up who tried to restore these very glories, but did not obtain them; but they prophesied of a day when this glory would be revealed. Paul spoke of the dispensation of the fulness of times, when God would gather together all things in one, etc.; and those men to whom these keys have been given, will have to be there; and they without us cannot be made perfect.

These men are in heaven, but their children are on the earth. Their bowels yearn over us. God sends down men for this reason. "And the Son of man shall send forth his angels, and they shall gather out of his kingdom all things that give offense and them that do iniquity"; (Matt. 13:41) All these authoritative characters will come down and join hand in hand in bringing about this work. (*D.H.C.* III, 388-389)

To Go Where God Is We Must Be like Him

. . . If you wish to go where God is, you must be like God, or possess the principles which God possesses, for if we are not drawing towards God in principle, we are going from him and drawing towards the devil. Yes, I am standing in the midst of all kinds of people.

Search your hearts, and see if you are like God. I have searched mine, and feel to repent of all my sins.

We have thieves among us, adulterers, liars, hypocrites. If God should speak from heaven, he would command you not to steal, not to commit adultery, not to covet, nor deceive, but be faithful over a few things. As far as we degenerate from God, we descend to the devil and lose knowledge, and without knowledge we cannot be saved, and while our hearts are filled with evil, and we are studying evil, there is no room in our hearts for good, or studying good. Is not God good? Then you be good; if he is faithful, then you be faithful. Add to your faith virtue, to virtue knowledge, and seek for every good thing. (*D.H.C.* IV, 588)

None Perfect but Jesus

. . . Where is the man that is free from vanity? None ever were perfect but Jesus; and why was he perfect? Because he was the Son of God, and had the fulness of the Spirit, and greater power than any man. But notwithstanding their vanity, men look forward with hope (because they are "subjected in hope") to the time of their deliverance. (*D.H.C.* IV, 358-359)

Three Independent Principles

May 16, 1841. "There are three independent principles; the Spirit of God, the spirit of man, and the spirit of the devil. All men have power to resist the devil.

"They who have tabernacles, have power over those who have not. The doctrine of eternal judgment; (Acts 2:41.) Peter preached, Repent, and be baptized in the name of Jesus Christ, for the remission of sins, etc.; but in Acts 3:19 he says, Repent and be converted, that your sins may be blotted out when the times of refreshing shall come, and he shall send Jesus, etc.

"Remission of sins by baptism was not to be preached to murderers. All the priests of Christendom might pray for a murderer on the scaffold forever, but could not avail so much as a gnat towards their forgiveness. There is no forgiveness for murderers; they will have to wait until the times of redemption shall come, and that in hell. Peter had the keys of eternal judgment, and he saw David in hell, and knew for what reason, and that David would have to remain there until the resurrection at the coming of Christ (Romans 9). All election that can be found in the scriptures is according to the flesh, and pertaining to the priesthood.

The Three Personages.—"Everlasting covenant was made between three personages before the organization of this earth, and relates to their dispensation of things to men on the earth: these personages, according to Abraham's record, are called God the first, the Creator; God the second, the Redeemer; and God the third, the witness or Testator." (Franklin D. Richards and Elder James A.

Little, *A Compendium of the Doctrines of the Gospel,*
1925 Edition, pp. 271-272)

All Mankind Are Capable of Growth

. . . All the minds and spirits that God ever sent into
the world are susceptible of enlargement. (*D.H.C.* VI, 311)

The One Hundred and Forty-four Thousand

. . . I remarked that the hundred and forty-four
thousand sealed are the priests who should be anointed
to administer in the daily sacrifice. (*D.H.C.* V, 326)

God Views All the Human Race as His Children

But while one portion of the human race is judging
and condemning the other without mercy, the Great Parent
of the universe looks upon the whole of the human family
with a fatherly care and paternal regard; he views them
as his offspring, and without any of those contracted feelings that influence the children of men, causes "his sun
to rise on the evil and on the good, and sendeth rain on the
just and on the unjust." (Matt. 5:45) He holds the reins of
judgment in his hands; he is a wise Lawgiver, and will judge
all men, not according to the narrow, contracted notions of
men, but, "according to the deeds done in the body
whether they be good or evil," or whether these deeds were
done in England, America, Spain, Turkey, or India. He
will judge them, "not according to what they have not,
but according to what they have," those who have lived
without law, will be judged without law, and those who
have a law, will be judged by that law. We need not doubt
the wisdom and intelligence of the Great Jehovah; he
will award judgment or mercy to all nations according to
their several deserts, their means of obtaining intelligence,
the laws by which they are governed, the facilities afforded
them of obtaining correct information, and his inscrutable

designs in relation to the human family; and when the designs of God shall be made manifest, and the curtain of futurity be withdrawn, we shall all of us eventually have to confess that the Judge of all the earth has done right. (*D.H.C.* IV, 595-596)

God a Self-existing Being, Man Exists upon like Principles

. . . The soul—the mind of man—the immortal spirit. Where did it come from? All learned men and doctors of divinity say that God created it in the beginning; but it is not so: the very idea lessens man in my estimation. I do not believe the doctrine; I know better. Hear it, all ye ends of the world; for God has told me so; and if you don't believe me, it will not make the truth without effect. I will make a man appear a fool before I get through; if he does not believe it. I am going to tell of things more noble.

We say that God himself is a self-existing being. Who told you so? It is correct enough; but how did it get into your heads? Who told you that man did not exist in like manner upon the same principles? Man does exist upon the same principles. God made a tabernacle and put a spirit into it, and it became a living soul. (Refers to the Bible.) How does it read in the Hebrew? It does not say in the Hebrew that God created the spirit of man. It says, "God made man out of the earth and put into him Adam's spirit, and so became a living body."

The mind or the intelligence which man possesses is co-equal [co-eternal] with God himself. (*D.H.C.* VI, 310)

In Order to Obtain Eternal Life We Must Know God

. . . The scriptures inform us that Jesus said, as the Father hath power in himself, even so hath the Son power —to do what? Why, what the Father did. The answer is

obvious—in a manner to lay down his body and take it up
again. Jesus, what are you going to do? To lay down my
life as my Father did, and take it up again. Do you believe
it? If you do not believe it you do not believe the Bible.
The scriptures say it, and I defy all the learning and wisdom and all the combined powers of earth and hell together to refute it. Here, then, is eternal life—to know the
only wise and true God; and you have got to learn how to
be gods yourselves, and to be kings and priests to God,
the same as all gods have done before you, namely, by
going from one small degree to another, and from a small
capacity to a great one; from grace to grace, from exaltation to exaltation, until you attain to the resurrection of
the dead, and are able to dwell in everlasting burnings,
and to sit in glory, as do those who sit enthroned in everlasting power. And I want you to know that God, in the
last days, while certain individuals are proclaiming his
name, is not trifling with you or me. (*D.H.C.* VI, 305-306)

The Great Secret

In the first place, I wish to go back to the beginning—
to the morn of creation. There is the starting point for us
to look to, in order to understand and be fully acquainted
with the mind, purposes and decrees of the Great Eloheim,
who sits in yonder heavens as he did at the creation of the
world. It is necessary for us to have an understanding of
God himself in the beginning. If we start right, it is easy
to go right all the time; but if we start wrong we may go
wrong, and it will be a hard matter to get right.

There are but a very few beings in the world who
understand rightly the character of God. The great majority of mankind do not comprehend anything, either that
which is past, or that which is to come, as it respects their
relationship to God. They do not know, neither do they
understand the nature of that relationship; and consequently they know but little above the brute beast, or more than

to eat, drink and sleep. This is all man knows about God or his existence, unless it is given by the inspiration of the Almighty.

If a man learns nothing more than to eat, drink and sleep, and does not comprehend any of the designs of God, the beast comprehends the same things. It eats, drinks, sleeps, and knows nothing more about God; yet it knows as much as we, unless we are able to comprehend by the inspiration of Almighty God. If men do not comprehend the character of God, they do not comprehend themselves. I want to go back to the beginning, and so lift your minds into more lofty spheres and a more exalted understanding than what the human mind generally aspires to.

I want to ask this congregation, every man, woman and child, to answer the question in their own hearts, what kind of a being God is? Ask yourselves; turn your thoughts into your hearts, and say if any of you have seen, heard, or communed with him? This is a question that may occupy your attention for a long time. I again repeat the question—What kind of being is God? Does any man or woman know? Have any of you seen him, heard him, or communed with him? Here is the question that will, peradventure, from this time henceforth occupy your attention. The scriptures inform us that "This is life eternal that they might know thee, the only true God, and Jesus Christ, whom thou hast sent." (John 17:3)

If any man does not know God, and inquires what kind of being he is—if he will search diligently his own heart—if the declaration of Jesus and the apostles be true, he will realize that he has not eternal life; for there can be eternal life on no other principle.

My first object is to find out the character of the only wise and true God, and what kind of being he is; and if I am so fortunate as to be the man to comprehend God, and explain or convey the principles to your hearts, so that the Spirit seals them upon you, then let every man and woman henceforth sit in silence, put their hands on their mouths, and never lift their hands or voices, or say anything against the man of God or the servants of God again. But if I fail to do it, it becomes my duty to renounce all further pretensions to revelations and inspirations, or to be a prophet; and I should be like the rest of the world— a false teacher, be hailed as a friend, and no man would seek my life. But if all religious teachers were honest enough to renounce their pretensions to godliness when their ignorance of the knowledge of God is made manifest, they will all be as badly off as I am, at any rate; and you might just as well take the lives of other false teachers as that of mine. If any man is authorized to take away my life because he thinks and says I am a false teacher, then, upon the same principle, we should be justified in taking away the life of every false teacher, and where would be the end of blood? And who would not be the sufferer? . . .

I will go back to the beginning before the world was, to show what kind of being God is. What sort of being was God in the beginning? Open your ears and hear, all ye ends of the earth, for I am going to prove it to you by the Bible, and to tell you the designs of God in relation to the human race, and why he interferes with the affairs of man.

God himself was once as we are now, and is an exalted man, and sits enthroned in yonder heavens! That is the great secret. If the veil were rent today, and the great God who holds this world in its orbit, and who upholds all worlds and all things by his power, was to make himself visible—I say, if you were to see him today, you would see him like a man in form—like yourselves in all the person, image, and very form as a man; for Adam was created in the very fashion, image and likeness of God, and received instruction from, and walked, talked, and conversed with him, as one man talks and communes with another. (*D.H.C.* VI, 303-305)

God Breathed into Adam the Breath of Life

The 7th verse of 2nd chapter of Genesis ought to read —God breathed into Adam his spirit [i.e. Adam's spirit] or breath of life; but when the word "rauch" applies to Eve, it should be translated lives. (*D.H.C.* V, 392-393)

How to Become Heirs of God

All men who become heirs of God and joint-heirs with Jesus Christ will have to receive the fulness of the ordinances of his kingdom; and those who will not receive all the ordinances will come short of the fulness of that glory, if they do not lose the whole. (*D.H.C.* V, 424)

Exaltation Promised to the Faithful

I do not regard my own life. I am ready to be offered a sacrifice for this people; for what can our enemies do? Only kill the body, and their power is then at an end! Stand firm, my friends; never flinch. Do not seek to save your lives, for he that is afraid to die for the truth, will lose eternal life. Hold out to the end, and we shall be resurrected and become like Gods, and reign in celestial kingdoms, principalities, and eternal dominions, while this cursed mob will sink to hell, the portion of all those who shed innocent blood. (*D.H.C.* VI, 500)

The Son Doeth What He Hath Seen the Father Do

If any man attempts to refute what I am about to say, after I have made it plain, let him beware.

As the Father hath power in himself, so hath the Son power in himself, to lay down his life and take it again, so he has a body of his own. The Son doeth what he hath seen the Father do: then the Father hath some day laid down his life and taken it again; so he has a body of his own; each one will be in his own body; and yet the sectarian world believe the body of the Son is identical with the Father's.

Gods have an ascendancy over the angels, who are ministering servants. In the resurrection, some are raised to be angels; others are raised to become Gods.

These things are revealed in the most holy place in a temple prepared for that purpose. . . . (*D.H.C.* V, 426-427)

God Dwells In Everlasting Burnings

God Almighty himself dwells in eternal fire; flesh and and blood cannot go there, for all corruption is devoured by the fire. "Our God is consuming fire." When our flesh is quickened by the Spirit, there will be no blood in this tabernacle. Some dwell in higher glory than others.

Those who have done wrong always have that wrong gnawing them. Immortality dwells in everlasting burnings. (*D.H.C.* VI, 366)

The Godhead

There is much said about God and the Godhead. The scriptures say there are Gods many and Lords Many, but to us there is but one living and true God, and the heaven of heavens could not contain him; for he took the liberty to go into other heavens. The teachers of the day say that the Father is God, the Son is God, and the Holy Ghost is God, and they are all in one body and one God. Jesus prayed that those that the Father had given him out of the world might be made one in them, as they were one; [one in spirit, in mind, in purpose]. If I were to testify that the Christian world were wrong on this point, my testimony would be true.

Peter and Stephen testify that they saw the Son of Man standing on the right hand of God. Any person that had seen the heavens opened knows that there are three personages in the heavens who hold the keys of power, and one presides over all. (*D.H.C.* V, 426)

The Two Comforters

There are two Comforters spoken of. One is the Holy Ghost, the same as given on the Day of Pentecost, and that all Saints receive after faith, repentance, and baptism. This first Comforter or Holy Ghost has no other effect than pure intelligence. It is more powerful in expanding the mind, enlightening the understanding, and storing the intellect with present knowledge, of a man who is of the literal seed of Abraham, than one that is a Gentile, though it may not have half as much visible effect upon the body; for as the Holy Ghost falls upon one of the literal seed of Abraham, it is calm and serene; and his whole soul and body are only exercised by the pure spirit of intelligence; while the effect of the Holy Ghost upon a Gentile is to purge out the old blood, and make him actually of the seed of Abraham. That man that has none of the blood of Abraham (naturally) must have a new creation by the Holy Ghost. In such a case, there may be more of a powerful effect upon the body, and visible to the eye, than upon an Israelite, while the Israelite at first might be far before the Gentile in pure intelligence.

The other Comforter spoken of is a subject of great interest, and perhaps understood by few of this generation. After a person has faith in Christ, repents of his sins, and is baptized for the remission of his sins and receives the Holy Ghost (by the laying on of hands), which is the first Comforter, then let him continue to humble himself before God, hungering and thirsting after righteousness, and living by every word of God, and the Lord will soon say unto him, Son, thou shalt be exalted. When the Lord has thoroughly proved him, and finds that the man is determined to serve Him at all hazards, then the man will find his calling and his election made sure, then it will be his privilege to receive the other Comforter, which the Lord hath promised the Saints, as is recorded in the testimony of John, in the 14th chapter, from the 12th to the 27th verses.

Note the 16, 17, 18, 21, 23 verses:

"16. And I will pray the Father, and he shall give you another Comforter, that he may abide with you for ever;

"17. Even the Spirit of truth; whom the world cannot receive, because it seeth him not, neither knoweth him: but ye know him; for he dwelleth with you, and shall be in you.

"18. I will not leave you comfortless: I will come to you. . . .

"21. He that hath my commandments, and keepeth them, he it is that loveth me: and he that loveth me shall be loved of my Father, and I will love him, and will manifest myself to him. . . .

"23. If a man love me, he will keep my words: and my Father will love him, and we will come unto him, and make our abode with him."

Now what is this other Comforter? It is no more nor less than the Lord Jesus Christ himself; and this is the sum and substance of the whole matter; that when any man obtains this last Comforter, he will have the personage of Jesus Christ to attend him, or appear unto him from time to time, and even he will manifest the Father unto him, and they will take up their abode with him, and the visions of the heavens will be opened unto him, and the Lord will teach him face to face, and he may have a perfect knowledge of the mysteries of the kingdom of God; and this is the state and place the ancient Saints arrived at when they had such glorious visions—Isaiah, Ezekiel, John upon the Isle of Patmos, Paul in the three heavens, and all the Saints who held communion with the general assembly and Church of the Firstborn. (*D.H.C.* III, 380-381)

Joint Heirship with Jesus Christ

Salem is designed for a Hebrew term. It should be *Shiloam,* which signified righteousness and peace: as it is, it is nothing—neither Hebrew, Greek, Latin, French, nor any other language.

I say to all those who are disposed to set up stakes for the Almighty, You will come short of the glory of God.

To become a joint heir of the heirship of the Son, one must put away all his false traditions. (*D.H.C.* V, 554)

Exaltation Explained

. . . How consoling to the mourners when they are called to part with a husband, wife, father, mother, child, or dear relative, to know that, although the earthly tabernacle is laid down and dissolved, they shall rise again to dwell in everlasting burnings in immortal glory, not to sorrow, suffer, or die any more, but they shall be heirs of God and joint heirs with Jesus Christ. What is it? To inherit the same power, the same glory and the same exaltation, until you arrive at the station of a God, and ascend the throne of eternal power, the same as those who have gone before. What did Jesus do? Why, I do the things I saw my Father do when worlds came rolling into existence. My Father worked out his kingdom with fear and trembling, and I must do the same; and when I get my kingdom, I shall present it to my Father, so that he may obtain kingdom upon kingdom, and it will exalt him in glory. He will then take a higher exaltation, and I will take his place, and thereby become exalted myself. So that Jesus treads in the tracks of his Father, and inherits what God did before; and God is thus glorified and exalted in the salvation and exaltation of all his children. It is plain beyond disputation, and you thus learn some of the first principles of the gospel, about which so much hath been said. (*D.H.C.* VI, 306)

A Council of the Gods

. . . I will go to the old Bible and turn commentator today.

I shall comment on the very first Hebrew word in the Bible; I will make a comment on the very first sentence of the history of creation in the Bible—*Berosheit*. I want to analyze the word. *Baith*—in, by, through, and everything else. *Roch*—the head, *Sheit*—grammatical termination. When the inspired man wrote it, he did not put the *baith* there. An old Jew without any authority added the word; he thought it too bad to talk about the head! It read first, "The head one of the Gods brought forth the Gods." That is the true meaning of the words. *Baurau* signifies to bring forth. . . .

. . . The head God called together the Gods and sat in grand council to bring forth the world. The grand councilors sat at the head in yonder heavens and contemplated the creation of the worlds, which were created at the time. . . .

In the beginning, the head of the Gods called a council of the Gods; and they came together and concocted [prepared] a plan to create the world and people it. When we begin to learn this way, we begin to learn the only true God, and what kind of being we have got to worship. Having a knowledge of God, we begin to know how to approach him, and how to ask so as to receive an answer.

When we understand the character of God, and know how to come to him, he begins to unfold the heavens to us, and to tell us all about it. When we are ready to come to him, he is ready to come to us.

Now I ask all who hear me, why learned men who are preaching salvation, say that God created the heavens and the earth out of nothing? The reason is, that they are unlearned in the things of God, and have not the gift of the Holy Ghost; they account it blasphemy in anyone to contradict their idea. If you tell them that God made the world out of something, they will call you a fool. But I am learned, and know more than all the world put together. The Holy Ghost does, anyhow, and he is within me, and comprehends more than all the world; and I will associate myself with him. (*D.H.C.* VI, 307-308)

A True Knowledge of God

The scriptures are a mixture of very strange doctrines to the Christian world, who are blindly led by the blind. I will refer to another scripture. "Now," says God, when he visited Moses in the bush, (Moses was a stammering sort of boy like me) God said, "Thou shalt be a God unto the children of Israel." God said, "Thou shalt be a God unto Aaron, and he shall be thy spokeman." I believe those Gods that God reveals as Gods to be sons of God, and all can cry, "Abba, Father!" Sons of God who exalt themselves to be Gods, even from before the foundation of the world, and are the only Gods I have a reverence for!

John said he was a king. "And from Jesus Christ, who is the faithful witness, and the first begotten of the dead, and the Prince of the kings of the earth. Unto him that loved us, and washed us from our sins in his own blood, and hath made us kings and priests unto God, and his Father; to him be glory and dominion forever and ever Amen." Oh, Thou God who art King of kings and Lord of lords, the sectarian world, by their actions, declare, "We cannot believe thee." (*D.H.C.* VI, 478)

Plurality of Gods

I will preach on the plurality of Gods. I have selected this text for that express purpose. I wish to declare I have always and in all congregations when I have preached on the subject of the Deity, it has been the plurality of Gods. It has been preached by the elders for fifteen years.

I have always declared God to be a distinct personage, Jesus Christ a separate and distinct personage from God the Father, and that the Holy Ghost was a distinct personage and a Spirit: and these three constitute three distinct personages and three Gods. If this is in accordance with the New Testament, lo and behold! we have three Gods anyhow, and they are plural: and who can contradict it?

Our text says "And hath made us kings and priests unto God and his Father." The apostles have discovered that there were Gods above, for Paul says God was the Father of our Lord Jesus Christ. My object was to preach the scriptures, and preach the doctrine they contain, there being a God above, the Father of our Lord Jesus Christ. I am bold to declare I have taught all the strong doctrines publicly, and always teach stronger doctrines in public than in private.

John was one of the men, and apostles declare they were made kings and priests unto God, the Father of our Lord Jesus Christ. It reads just so in the revelation. Hence, the doctrine of a plurality of Gods is as prominent in the Bible as any other doctrine. It is all over the face of the Bible. It stands beyond the power of controversy. A wayfaring man, though a fool, need not err therein.

Paul says there are Gods many and Lords many. I want to set it forth in a plain and simple manner; but to us there is but one God—that is *pertaining to us;* and he is in all and through all. But if Joseph Smith says there are Gods many and Lords many, they cry, "Away with him! Crucify him! crucify him!"

Mankind verily says that the scriptures are with them. Search the scriptures, for they testify of things that these apostates would gravely pronounce blasphemy. Paul, if Joseph Smith is a blasphemer, you are. I say there are Gods many and Lords many, but to us only one, and we are to be in subjection to that one, and no man can limit the bounds or the eternal existence of eternal time. Hath he beheld the eternal world, and is he authorized to say that there is only one God? He makes himself a fool if he thinks or says so, and there is an end of his career or progress in knowledge. He cannot obtain all knowledge, for he has sealed up the gate to it.

Some say I do not interpret the scripture the same as they do. They say it means the heathen's gods. Paul says there are Gods many and Lords many; and that makes a plurality of Gods, in spite of the whims of all men. Without a revelation, I am not going to give them the knowledge of the God of heaven. You know and I testify that Paul had no allusion to the heathen gods. I have it from God, and get over it if you can. I have a witness of the Holy Ghost, and a testimony that Paul had no allusion to the heathen gods in the text. I will show from the Hebrew Bible that I am correct, and the first word shows a plurality of Gods; and I want the apostates and learned men to come here and prove to the contrary, if they can. An unlearned boy must give you a little Hebrew. *Berosheit baurau Eloheim ait aushamayeen vehau auraits,* rendered by King James' translators, "In the beginning God created the heaven and the earth." I want to analyze the word *Berosheit. Rosh,* the head; *Sheit,* a grammatical termination, the *Baith* was not originally put there when the inspired man wrote it, but it has been since added by an old Jew. *Baurau* signified to bring forth; *Eloheim* is from the word *Eloi,* God, in the singular number; and by adding the word *heim,* it renders it Gods. It read first, "In the beginning the head of the Gods brought forth the Gods," or, as others have translated it, "The head of the Gods called the Gods together." I want to show a little learning as well as other fools—

A little learning is a dangerous thing.
Drink deep, or taste not the Pierian spring,
There shallow draughts intoxicate the brain,
And drinking largely sobers us up again.

All this confusion among professed translators is for want of drinking another draught.

The head God organized the heavens and the earth.
I defy all the world to refute me. In the beginning the
heads of the Gods organized the heavens and the earth.
Now the learned priests and the people rage, and the
heathen imagine a vain thing. If we pursue the Hebrew
text further, it reads, *"Berosheit baurau Eloheim ait
aashamayeen vehau auraits."*—"The head one of the Gods
said, Let us make a man in our own image." I once asked
a learned Jew, "If the Hebrew language compels us to
render all words ending in *heim* in the plural, why not
render the first *Eloheim* plural?" He replied, "That is the
rule with few exceptions; but in this case it would ruin
the Bible." He acknowledged I was right. I came here
to investigate these things precisely as I believe them.
Hear and judge for yourselves; and if you go away satisfied,
well and good.

In the very beginning the Bible shows there is a
plurality of Gods beyond the power of refutation. It is a
great subject I am dwelling on. The word *Eloheim* ought
to be in the plural all the way through—Gods. The heads
of the Gods appointed one God for us; and when you take
[that] view of the subject, it sets one free to see all the
beauty, holiness and perfection of the Gods. All I want is
to get the simple, naked truth, and the whole truth.

Many men say there is one God; the Father, the Son
and the Holy Ghost are only one God! I say that is a
strange God anyhow—three in one, and one in three! It
is a curious organization. "Father, I pray not for the world,
but I pray for them which thou hast given me." "Holy
Father, keep through thine own name those whom thou
hast given me, that they may be one as we are." All are
to be crammed into one God, according to sectarianism.
It would make the biggest God in all the world. He would
be a wonderfully big God—he would be a giant or a mon-
ster. I want to read the text to you myself—"I am agreed
with the Father and the Father is agreed with me, and we
are agreed as one." The Greek shows that it should be

agreed. "Father, I pray for them which thou hast given me out of the world, and not for those alone, but for them also which shall believe on me through their word, that they all may be agreed, as thou, Father, art with me, and I with thee, that they also may be agreed with us," and all come to dwell in unity, and in all the glory and everlasting burnings of the Gods; and then we shall see as we are seen, and be as our God and he as his Father. I want to reason a little on this subject. I learned it by translating the papyrus which is now in my house. I learned a testimony concerning Abraham, and he reasoned concerning the God of heaven. "In order to do that," said he, "suppose we have two facts: that supposes another fact may exist—two men on the earth, one wiser than the other, would logically show that another who is wiser than the wisest may exist. Intelligences exist one above another, so that there is no end to them."

If Abraham reasoned thus—If Jesus Christ was the Son of God, and John discovered that God the Father of Jesus Christ had a Father, you may suppose that he had a Father also. Where was there ever a son without a father? And where was there ever a father without first being a son? Whenever did a tree or anything spring into existence without a progenitor? And everything comes in this way. Paul says that which is earthly is in the likeness of that which is heavenly, hence if Jesus had a Father, can we not believe that *he* had a Father also? I despise the idea of being scared to death at such a doctrine, for the Bible is full of it.

I want you to pay particular attention to what I am saying. Jesus said that the Father wrought precisely in the same way as his Father had done before him. As the Father had done before. He laid down his life, and took it up the same as his Father had done before. He did as he was sent, to lay down his life and take it up again; and then was committed unto him the keys, etc. I know it is good reasoning. . . .

They found fault with Jesus Christ because he said he was the Son of God, and made himself equal with God. They say of me, as they did of the apostles of old, that I must be put down. What did Jesus say? "Is it not written in your law, I said, Ye are Gods? If he called them Gods unto whom the word of God came, and the scriptures cannot be broken, say ye of him whom the Father had sanctified and sent into the world, Thou blasphemest, because I said I am the Son of God?" It was through him that they drank of the spiritual rock. Of course he would take the honor to himself. Jesus, if they were called Gods unto whom the word of God came, why should it be thought blasphemy that I should say I am the Son of God? (*D.H.C.* VI, 474-477)

Certain Gospel Principles Not to Be Comprehended in This Life

When you climb up a ladder, you must begin at the bottom, and ascend step by step, until you arrive at the top; and so it is with the principles of the gospel—you must begin with the first, and go on until you learn all the principles of exaltation. But it will be a great while after you have passed through the veil before you will have learned them. It is not all to be comprehended in this world; it will be a great work to learn our salvation and exaltation even beyond the grave. (*D.H.C.* VI, 306-307)

CHAPTER TWO

Priesthood

Priesthood and the Keys of the Priesthood

The priesthood was first given to Adam; he obtained the First Presidency, and held the keys of it from generation to generation. He obtained it in the Creation, before the world was formed, as in Gen. 1:26-28. He had dominion given him over every living creature. He is Michael the Archangel, spoken of in the scriptures. Then to Noah, who is Gabriel; he stands next in authority to Adam in the priesthood; he was called of God to this office, and was the father of all living in his day, and to him was given the dominion. These men held keys first on earth, and then in heaven. (*D.H.C.* III, 385-386)

Eternity of the Priesthood

The priesthood is an everlasting principle, and existed with God from eternity, and will to eternity, without beginning of days or end of years. The keys have to be brought from heaven whenever the Gospel is sent. When they are revealed from heaven, it is by Adam's authority. . . .

The priesthood is everlasting. The Savior, Moses, and Elias, gave the keys to Peter, James, and John, on the mount, when they were transfigured before him. The priesthood is everlasting—without beginning of days or end of years; without father, mother, etc. If there is no change of ordinances, there is no change of priesthood. Wherever the ordinances of the Gospel are administered, there is the priesthood.

How have we come at the priesthood in the last days?
It came down, down, in regular succession. Peter, James,
and John had it given to them and they gave it to others.
Christ is the Great High Priest; Adam next. (*D.H.C.* III,
386, 387, 388)

All Priesthood Is Melchizedek

Different Degrees of the Priesthood of Melchizedek.

"Answer to the question, Was the priesthood of Melchizedek taken away when Moses died? All priesthood
is Melchizedek, but there are different portions or degrees
of it. That portion which brought Moses to speak with
God face to face was taken away; but that which brought
the ministry of angels remained. All the prophets had the
Melchizedek Priesthood and were ordained by God
himself. (Franklin D. Richards and Elder James A. Little,
A Compendium of the Doctrines of the Gospel, 1925
Edition, pp. 270-271)

Three Grand Orders of Priesthood

There are three grand orders of priesthood . . .

1st. The King of Shiloam. (Salem) had power and
authority over that of Abraham, holding the key and the
power of endless life. Angels desire to look into it, but they
have set up too many stakes. God cursed the children of
Israel because they would not receive the last law from
Moses.

The sacrifice required of Abraham in the offering up
of Isaac, shows that if a man would attain to the keys of
the kingdom of an endless life; he must sacrifice all things.
When God offers a blessing or knowledge to a man, and
he refuses to receive it, he will be damned. The Israelites
prayed that God would speak to Moses and not to them;
in consequence of which he cursed them with a carnal
law.

What was the power of Melchizedek? 'Twas not the Priesthood of Aaron which administers in outward ordinances, and the offering of sacrifices. Those holding the fulness of the Melchizedek Priesthood are kings and priests of the Most High God, holding the keys of power and blessings. In fact, that priesthood is a perfect law of theocracy, and stands as God to give laws to the people, administering endless lives to the sons and daughters of Adam.

Abraham says to Melchizedek, I believe all that thou hast taught me concerning the priesthood and the coming of the Son of Man; so Melchizedek ordained Abraham and sent him away. Abraham rejoiced, saying, Now I have a priesthood.

Salvation could not come to the world without the mediation of Jesus Christ.

How shall God come to the rescue of this generation? He will send Elijah the prophet. The law revealed to Moses in Horeb never was revealed to the children of Israel as a nation.

Elijah shall reveal the covenants to seal the hearts of the fathers to the children, and the children to the fathers.

The anointing and sealing is to be called, elected and made sure.

"Without father, without mother, without descent, having neither beginning of days nor end of life, but made like unto the Son of God, abideth a priest continually." The Melchizedek Priesthood holds the right from the eternal God, and not by descent from father and mother; and that priesthood is as eternal as God himself, having neither beginning of days nor end of life.

The 2nd priesthood is patriarchal authority. Go to and finish the temple, and God will fill it with power, and you will then receive more knowledge concerning this priesthood.

The 3rd is what is called the Levitical Priesthood, consisting of priests to administer in outward ordinance, made without an oath; but the priesthood of Melchizedek is by an oath and covenant.

The Holy Ghost is God's messenger to administer in all those priesthoods.

Jesus Christ is the heir of this kingdom—the Only Begotten of the Father according to the flesh, and holds the keys over all this world.

Men have to suffer that they may come upon Mount Zion and be exalted above the heavens.

I know a man that has been caught up to the third heavens, and can say, with Paul, that we have seen and heard things that are not lawful to utter. (*D.H.C.* V, 554-556)

How to Obtain a Fulness of the Priesthood of God

If a man gets a fulness of the priesthood of God, he has to get it in the same way that Jesus Christ obtained it, and that was by keeping all the commandments and obeying all the ordinances of the house of the Lord.

Where there is no change of priesthood, there is no change of ordinances, says Paul, if God has not changed the ordinances and the priesthood. Howl, ye sectarians! If he has, when and where has he revealed it? Have ye turned revelators? Then why deny revelation? (*D.H.C.* V, 424)

Priesthood

In order to investigate the subject of the priesthood, so important to this, as well as every succeeding generation, I shall proceed to trace the subject as far as I possibly can from the Old and New Testaments.

There are two priesthoods spoken of in the scriptures, viz., the Melchisedek and the Aaronic or Levitical. Although there are two priesthoods, yet the Melchisedek

Priesthood comprehends the Aaronic or Levitical Priesthood, and is the grand head, and holds the highest authority which pertains to the priesthood, and the keys of the kingdom of God in all ages of the world to the latest posterity on the earth, and is the channel through which all knowledge, doctrine, the plan of salvation, and every important matter is revealed from heaven.

Its institution was prior to "the foundation of this earth, or the morning stars sang together, or the Sons of God shouted for joy," and is the highest and holiest priesthood, and is after the order of the Son of God, and all other priesthoods are only parts, ramifications, powers and blessings belonging to the same, and are held, controlled, and directed by it. It is the channel through which the Almighty commenced revealing his glory at the beginning of the creation of this earth, and through which he has continued to reveal himself to the children of men to the present time, and through which he will make known his purposes to the end of time.

Commencing with Adam, who was the first man, who is spoken of in Daniel as being the "Ancient of Days," or in other words, the first and oldest of all, the great, grand progenitor of whom it is said in another place he is Michael, because he was the first and father of all, not only by progeny, but the first to hold the spiritual blessings, to whom was made known the plan of ordinances for the salvation of his posterity unto the end, and to whom Christ was first revealed, and through whom Christ has been revealed from heaven, and will continue to be revealed from henceforth. Adam holds the keys of the Dispensation of the Fulness of Times; i.e., the dispensation of all the times have been and will be revealed through him from the beginning to Christ, and from Christ to the end of all the dispensations that are to be revealed. "Having made known unto us the mystery of his will, according to his good pleasure which he hath purposed in himself: that in the Dispensation of the Fulness of Times he might gather together in one all things in Christ, both which are in heaven, and which are on earth; even in him." (Eph. 1:9-10)

Now the purpose in himself in the winding up scene of the last dispensation is that all things pertaining to that dispensation should be conducted precisely in accordance with the preceding dispensations.

And again, God purposed in himself that there should not be an eternal fulness until every dispensation should be fulfilled and gathered together in one, and that all things whatsoever, that should be gathered together in one in those dispensations unto the same fulness and eternal glory, should be in Christ Jesus; therefore he set the ordinances to be the same forever and ever, and set Adam to watch over them, to reveal them from heaven to man, or to send angels to reveal them. "Are they not all ministering spirits, sent forth to minister for them who shall be heirs of salvation?" (Heb. 1:14)

These angels are under the direction of Michael or Adam, who acts under the direction of the Lord. From the above quotation we learn that Paul perfectly understood the purposes of God in relation to his connection with man, and that glorious and perfect order which he established in himself, whereby he sent forth power, revelations, and glory.

God will not acknowledge that which he has not called, ordained, and chosen. In the beginning God called Adam by his own voice. "And the Lord called unto Adam and said unto him, Where art thou? And he said, I heard thy voice in the garden, and I was afraid because I was naked and hid myself." (See Gen. 3:9-10.) Adam received commandments and instructions from God: this was the order from the beginning.

That he received revelations, commandments and ordinances at the beginning is beyond the power of controversy; else how did they begin to offer sacrifices to God in an acceptable manner? And if they offered sacrifices

they must be authorized by ordination. We read in Genesis, (4:4), that Abel brought of the firstlings of the
flock and the fat thereof, and the Lord had respect
to Abel and to his offering. And again, "By faith Abel
offered unto God a more excellent sacrifice than Cain, by
which he obtained witness that he was righteous, God
testifying of his gifts; and by it he being dead, yet speaketh." (Heb. 11:4) How doth he yet speak? Why
he magnified the priesthood which was conferred upon
him, and died a righteous man, and therefore has become
an angel of God by receiving his body from the dead,
holding still the keys of his dispensation; and was sent
down from heaven unto Paul to minister consoling words,
and to commit unto him a knowledge of the mysteries of
godliness.

And if this was not the case, I would ask, how did
Paul know so much about Abel, and who should he talk
about his speaking after he was dead? Hence, that he
spoke after he was dead must be by being sent down out
of heaven to adminster.

This, then, is the nature of the priesthood; every man
holding the presidency of his dispensation, and one man
holding the presidency of them all, even Adam; and Adam
receiving his presidency and authority from the Lord, but
cannot receive a fulness until Christ shall present the
Kingdom to the Father, which shall be at the end of the
last dispensation.

The power, glory and blessings of the priesthood could
not continue with those who received ordination only as
their righteousness continued; for Cain also being authorized to offer sacrifice, but not offering it in righteousness,
was cursed. It signified, then, that the ordinances must
be kept in the very way God has appointed; otherwise their
priesthood will prove a cursing instead of a blessing.

If Cain had fulfilled the law of righteousness as did
Enoch, he could have walked with God all the days of
his life, and never failed of a blessing. "And Enoch walked

with God after he begat Methuselah 300 years, and begat sons and daughters, and all the days of Enoch were 365 years; and Enoch walked with God, and he was not, for God took him." (Gen. 5:22) Now this Enoch God reserved unto himself, that he should not die at that time, and appointed unto him a ministry unto terrestrial bodies, of whom there has been but little revealed. He is reserved also unto the presidency of a dispensation, and more shall be said of him and terrestrial bodies in another treatise. He is a ministering angel, to minister to those who shall be heirs of salvation, and appeared unto Jude as Abel did unto Paul; therefore Jude spoke of him. (*Ibid.*, 14-15) And Enoch, the seventh from Adam, revealed these sayings: "Behold, the Lord cometh with ten thousand of his Saints."

Paul was also acquainted with this character, and received instructions from him. "By faith Enoch was translated, that he should not see death; and was not found, because God had translated him: for before his translation he had this testimony, that he pleased God; But without faith, it is impossible to please him: for he that cometh to God must believe that he is, and that he is a rewarder of those who diligently seek him." (Heb. 11:5)

Now the doctrine of translation is a power which belongs to this priesthood. There are many things which belong to the powers of the priesthood and the keys thereof, that have been kept hid from before the foundation of the world; they are hid from the wise and prudent to be revealed in the last times.

Many have supposed that the doctrine of translation was a doctrine whereby men were taken immediately into the presence of God, and into an eternal fulness, but this is a mistaken idea. Their place of habitation is that of the terrestrial order, and a place prepared for such characters he held in reserve to be ministering angels unto many planets, and who as yet have not entered into so great a fulness as those who are resurrected from the dead.

"Others were tortured, not accepting deliverance, that they might obtain a better resurrection:" (See Heb. 11:35.)

Now it was evident that there was a better resurrection, or else God would not have revealed it unto Paul. Wherein then, can it be said a better resurrection? This distinction is made between the doctrine of the actual resurrection and translation: translation obtains deliverance from the tortures and sufferings of the body, but their existence will prolong as to the labors and toils of the ministry, before they can enter into so great a rest and glory.

On the other hand, those who were tortured, not accepting deliverance, received an immediate rest from their labors. "And I heard a voice from heaven, saying unto me, Write, Blessed are the dead which die in the Lord, from henceforth: . . . they may rest from their labours and their works do follow them." (Rev. 14:13)

They rest from their labors for a long time, and yet their work is held in reserve for them, that they are permitted to do the same work, after they receive a resurrection for their bodies. But we shall leave this subject and the subject of the terrestrial bodies for another time, in order to treat upon them more fully.

The next great, grand patriarch [after Enoch] who held the keys of the priesthood was Lamech. "And Lamech lived one hundred eighty and two years and begat a son: and he called his name Noah, saying, This same shall comfort us concerning our work and the toil of our hands because of the ground which the Lord hath cursed." (Gen. 5:28-29) The priesthood continued from Lamech to Noah: "And God said unto Noah, The end of all flesh is before me; for the earth is filled with violence through them; and, behold, I will destroy them with the earth." (Gen. 6:13)

Thus we behold the keys of this priesthood consisted in obtaining the voice of Jehovah that he talked with him [Noah] in a familiar and friendly manner, that he continued to him the keys, the covenants, the power and the glory, with which he blessed Adam at the beginning; and the offering of sacrifice, which also shall be continued at the last time; for all the ordinances and duties that ever have been required by the priesthood, under the directions and commandments of the Almighty in any of the dispensations, shall all be had in the last dispensation, therefore all things had under the authority of the priesthood at any former period, shall be had again, bringing to pass the restoration spoken of by the mouth of all the holy prophets; then shall the sons of Levi offer an acceptable offering to the Lord. "And he shall sit as a refiner and purifier of silver: and he shall purify the sons of Levi, and purge them as gold and silver, that they may offer unto the Lord." (See Mal. 3:3.)

It will be necessary here to make a few observations on the doctrine set forth in the above quotation, and it is generally supposed that sacrifice was entirely done away when the Great Sacrifice [i.e., the sacrifice of the Lord Jesus] was offered up, and that there will be no necessity for the ordinance of sacrifice in future: but those who assert this are certainly not acquainted with the duties, privileges and authority of the priesthood, or with the prophets.

The offering of sacrifice has ever been connected and forms a part of the duties of the priesthood. It began with the priesthood and will be continued until after the coming of Christ, from generation to generation. We frequently have mention made of the offering of sacrifice by the servants of the Most High in ancient days, prior to the law of Moses; which ordinances will be continued when the priesthood is restored with all its authority, power and blessings.

Elijah was the last prophet that held the keys of the priesthood, and who will, before the last dispensation, restore the authority and deliver the keys of the priesthood, in order that all the ordinances may be attended to in righteousness. It is true that the Savior had authority and power to bestow this blessing; but the sons of Levi were too prejudiced. "And I will send Elijah the Prophet before the great and terrible day of the Lord," etc., etc. Why send Elijah? Because he holds the keys of the authority to administer in all the ordinances of the priesthood; and without the authority is given, the ordinances could not be administered in righteousness.

It is a very prevalent opinion that the sacrifices which were offered were entirely consumed. This was not the case; if you read Leviticus, 2:2-3, you will observe that the priests took a part as a memorial and offered it up before the Lord, while the remainder was kept for the maintenance of the priests; so that the offerings and sacrifices are not all consumed upon the altar—but the blood is sprinkled, and the fat and certain other portions are consumed.

These sacrifices, as well as every ordinance belonging to the priesthood, will, when the temple of the Lord shall be built, and the sons of Levi be purified, be fully restored and attended to in all their powers, ramifications, and blessings. This ever did and ever will exist when the powers of the Melchizedek Priesthood are sufficiently manifest; else how can the restitution of all things spoken of by the holy prophets be brought to pass? It is not to be understood that the law of Moses will be established again with all its rites and variety of ceremonies; this has never been spoken of by the prophets; but those things which existed prior to Moses' day, namely, sacrifice, will be continued.

It may be asked by some, what necessity for sacrifice, since the Great Sacrifice was offered? In answer to which, if repentance, baptism, and faith existed prior to the days of Christ, what necessity for them since that time? The priesthood has descended in a regular line from father to son, through their succeeding generations. (D.H.C. IV, 207-212)

The Priesthood

Respecting the Melchizedek Priesthood, the sectarians never professed to have it; consequently they never could save anyone, and would all be damned together. There was an Episcopal priest who said he had the priesthood of Aaron, but had not the priesthood of Melchizedek: and I bear testimony that I never have found the man who claimed the priesthood of Melchizedek. The power of the Melchizedek Priesthood is to have the power of "endless lives"; for the everlasting covenant cannot be broken.

The law was given under Aaron for the purpose of pouring out judgments and destructions. (*D.H.C.* V, 554)

Women to Receive Instruction through the Priesthood

You will receive instructions through the order of the priesthood which God has established, through the medium of those appointed to lead, guide and direct the affairs of the Church in this last dispensation; and I now turn the key in your behalf in the name of the Lord, and this [Relief] Society shall rejoice, and knowledge and intelligence shall flow down from this time henceforth; this is the beginning of better days to the poor and needy, who shall be made to rejoice and pour forth blessings on your heads. (*D.H.C.* IV, 607)

Discourse on the Spirit and Work of Elias, Elijah, Messiah

There is a difference between the spirit and office of Elias and Elijah. It is the spirit of Elias I wish first to speak of; and in order to come at the subject, I will bring some of the testimony from the scripture and give my own.

In the first place, suffice it to say, I went into the woods to inquire of the Lord, by prayer, his will concerning me, and I saw an angel, and he laid his hands upon my head, and ordained me to a priest after the order of Aaron, and to hold the keys of this priesthood, which office was to preach repentance and baptism for the remission of sins, and also to baptize. But I was informed that this office did not extend to the laying on of hands for the giving of the Holy Ghost; that that office was a greater work, and was to be given afterward; but that my ordination was a preparatory work, or a going before, which was the spirit of Elias; for the spirit of Elias was a going before to prepare the way for the greater, which was the case with John the Baptist. He came crying through the wilderness, "Prepare ye the way of the Lord, make his paths straight." And they were informed, if they could receive it, it was the spirit of Elias; and John was very particular to tell the people, he was not that Light, but was sent to bear witness of that Light.

He told the people that his mission was to preach repentance and baptize with water; but it was he that should come after him that should baptize with fire and the Holy Ghost.

If he had been an impostor, he might have gone to work beyond his bounds, and undertaken to have performed ordinances which did not belong to that office and calling, under the spirit of Elias.

The spirit of Elias is to prepare the way for a greater revelation of God, which is the priesthood of Elias, or the priesthood that Aaron was ordained unto. And when God sends a man into the world to prepare for a greater work, holding the keys of the power of Elias, it was called the doctrine of Elias, even from the early ages of the world.

John's mission was limited to preaching and baptizing; but what he did was legal; and when Jesus Christ came to any of John's disciples, he baptized them with fire and the Holy Ghost.

We find the apostles endowed with greater power than John: their office was more under the spirit and power of Elijah than Elias.

In the case of Philip when he went down to Samaria, when he was under the spirit of Elias, he baptized both men and women. When Peter and John heard of it, they went down and laid hands upon them, and they received the Holy Ghost. This shows the distinction between the two powers.

When Paul came to certain disciples, he asked if they had received the Holy Ghost? They said, No. Who baptized you, then? We were baptized unto John's baptism. No, you were not baptized unto John's baptism, or you would have been baptized by John. And so Paul went and baptized them, for he knew what the true doctrine was, and he knew that John had not baptized them. And these principles are strange to me, that men who have read the scriptures of the New Testament are so far from it.

What I want to impress upon your minds is the difference of power in the different parts of the priesthood, so that when any man comes among you, saying, "I have the spirit of Elias," you can know whether he be true or false; for any man that comes, having the spirit and power of Elias, he will not transcend his bounds.

John did not transcend his bounds, but faithfully performed that part belonging to his office; and every portion of the great building should be prepared right and assigned to its proper place; and it is necessary to know who holds the keys of power, and who does not, or we may be likely to be deceived.

That person who holds the keys of Elias hath a preparatory work. But if I spend much more time in conversing about the spirit of Elias, I shall not have time to do justice to the spirit and power of Elijah.

This is the Elias spoken of in the last days, and here is the rock upon which many split, thinking the time was past in the days of John and Christ, and no more to be. But the spirit of Elias was revealed to me, and I know it is true; therefore I speak with boldness, for I know verily my doctrine is true.

Now for Elijah. The spirit, power, and calling of Elijah is, that ye have power to hold the key of the revelation, ordinances, oracles, powers and endowments of the fulness of the Melchizedek Priesthood and of the kingdom of God on the earth; and to receive, obtain, and perform all the ordinances belonging to the kingdom of God, even unto the turning of the hearts of the fathers unto the children, and the hearts of the children unto the fathers, even those who are in heaven.

Malachi says, ". . . I will send you Elijah the prophet before the coming of the great and dreadful day of the Lord: And he shall turn the heart of the fathers to the children, and the heart of the children to their fathers, lest I come and smite the earth with a curse." (Mal. 4:5-6)

Now, what I am after is the knowledge of God, and I take my own course to obtain it. What are we to understand by this in the last days?

In the days of Noah, God destroyed the world by a flood, and he has promised to destroy it by fire in the last days: but before it should take place, Elijah should first come and turn the hearts of the fathers to the children, etc.

Now comes the point. What is this office and work of Elijah? It is one of the greatest and most important subjects that God has revealed. He should send Elijah to seal the children to the fathers, and the fathers to the children.

Now was this merely confined to the living, to settle difficulties with families on earth? By no means. It was a far greater work. Elijah! what would you do if you were here? Would you confine your work to the living alone? No: I would refer you to the scriptures, where the subject is manifest: that is, without us, they could not be made perfect, nor we without them; the fathers without the children, nor the children without the fathers.

I wish you to understand this subject, for it is important; and if you will receive it, this is the spirit of Elijah, that we redeem our dead, and connect ourselves with our fathers which are in heaven, and seal up our dead to come forth in the first resurrection; and here we want the power

of Elijah to seal those who dwell on earth to those who
dwell in heaven. This is the power of Elijah and the keys
of the kingdom of Jehovah.

Let us suppose a case. Suppose the great God who
dwells in heaven should reveal himself to Father Cutler
here, by the opening heavens, and tell him, "I offer up
a decree that whatsoever you seal on earth with your
decree, I will seal it in heaven." You have the power then;
can it be taken off? No. Then what you seal on earth, by
the keys of Elijah, is sealed in heaven; and this is the power
of Elijah, and this is the difference between the spirit and
power of Elias and Elijah; for while the spirit of Elias is
a forerunner, the power of Elijah is sufficient to make
our calling and election sure; and the same doctrine, where
we are exhorted to go on to perfection, not laying again
the foundation of repentance from dead works, and of
laying on of hands, resurrection of the dead, etc.

We cannot be perfect without the fathers, etc. We
must have revelation from them, and we can see that the
doctrine of revelation far transcends the doctrine of no
revelation; for one truth revealed from heaven is worth
all the sectarian notions in existence.

This spirit of Elijah was manifest in the days of the
apostles, in delivering certain ones to the buffetings of
Satan, that they might be saved in the day of the Lord
Jesus. They were sealed by the spirit of Elijah unto the
damnation of hell until the day of the Lord, or revelation
of Jesus Christ.

Here is the doctrine of election that the world has
quarreled so much about; but they do not know anything
about it.

The doctrine that the Presbyterians and Methodists
have quarreled so much about—once in grace, always in
grace, or falling away from grace, I will say a word about.
They are both wrong. Truth takes a road between them
both, for while the Presbyterian says "once in grace, you
cannot fall"; the Methodist says: "You can have grace to-

day, fall from it tomorrow, next day have grace again; and so follow on, changing continually." But the doctrine of the scriptures and the spirit of Elijah would show them both false, and take a road between them both; for, according to the scripture, if men have received the good word of God, and tasted of the powers of the world to come, if they shall fall away, it is impossible to renew them again, seeing they have crucified the Son of God afresh, and put him to an open shame; so there is a possibility of falling away; you could not be renewed again, and the power of Elijah cannot seal against this sin, for this is a reserve made in the seals and power of the priesthood.

I will make every doctrine plain that I present, and it shall stand upon a firm basis, and I am at the defiance of the world, for I will take shelter under the broad cover of the wings of the work in which I am engaged. It matters not to me if all hell boils over; I regard it only as I would the crackling of the thorns under a pot.

A murderer, for instance, one that sheds innocent blood, cannot have forgiveness. David sought repentance at the hand of God carefully with tears, for the murder of Uriah; but he could only get it through hell: he got a promise that his soul should not be left in hell.

Although David was a king, he never did obtain the spirit and power of Elijah and the fulness of the priesthood; and the priesthood that he received, and the throne and kingdom of David is to be taken from him and given to another by the name of David in the last days, raised up out of his lineage.

Peter referred to the same subject on the Day of Pentecost, but the multitude did not get the endowment that Peter had; but several days after, the people asked "What shall we do?" Peter says, "I would ye had done it ignorantly," speaking of crucifying the Lord, etc. He did not say to them, "Repent and be baptized, for the remission of your sins"; but he said, "Repent ye therefore, and be converted, that your sins may be blotted out, when the times of refreshing shall come from the presence of the Lord"; (Acts 3:19)

This is the case with murderers. They could not be baptized for the remission of sins for they had shed innocent blood.

Again: The doctrine or sealing power of Elijah is as follows:—If you have power to seal on earth and in heaven, then we should be wise. The first thing you do, go and seal on earth your sons and daughters unto yourself, and yourself unto your fathers in eternal glory. . . . I will walk through the gate of heaven and claim what I seal, and those that follow me and my counsel.

The Lord once told me that what I asked for I should have. I have been afraid to ask God to kill my enemies, lest some of them should, peradventure, repent.

I asked a short time since for the Lord to deliver me out of the hands of the Governor of Missouri, and if it needs must be to accomplish it, to take him away; and the next news that came pouring down from there was, that *Governor Reynolds had shot himself.* And I would now say, "Beware, O earth, how you fight against the Saints of God and shed innocent blood; for in the days of Elijah, his enemies came upon him, and fire was called down from heaven and destroyed them."

The spirit of Elias is first, Elijah second, and Messiah last. Elias is a forerunner to prepare the way, and the spirit and power of Elijah is to come after, holding the keys of power, building the temple to the capstone, placing the seals of the Melchizedek Priesthood upon the house of Israel, and making all things ready; then Messiah comes to his temple, which is last of all.

Messiah is above the spirit and power of Elijah, for he made the world, and was that spiritual rock unto Moses in the wilderness. Elijah was to come and prepare the way and build up the kingdom before the coming of the great day of the Lord, although the spirit of Elias might begin it. . . . (*D.H.C.* VI, 249-254)

CHAPTER THREE

Revelation

The Church Built upon the Rock of Revelation

John was a priest after the order of Aaron, and had the keys of that priesthood, and came forth preaching repentance and baptism for the remission of sins, but at the same time cried out, "There cometh one mightier than I after me, the latchet of whose shoes I am not worthy to stoop down and unloose," and Christ came according to the words of John, and he was greater than John, because he held the keys of the Melchizedek Priesthood and kingdom of God, and had before revealed the priesthood of Moses, yet Christ was baptized by John to fulfil all righteousness; and Jesus in his teachings says, "Upon this rock I will build my Church, and the gates of hell shall not prevail against it." What rock? Revelation. (*D.H.C.* V, 258)

Revelation Is a Privilege of the Priesthood

. . . one great privilege of the priesthood is to obtain revelations of the mind and will of God. It is also the privilege of the Melchizedek Priesthood, to reprove, rebuke, and admonish, as well as to receive revelation. (*D.H.C.* II, 477)

Special Revelation and How Obtained

. . . we never inquire at the hand of God for special revelation only in case of there being no previous revelation to suit the case; and that in a council of high priests. . . .

It is a great thing to inquire at the hands of God, or to come into his presence; and we feel fearful to approach

him on subjects that are of little or no consequence, to
satisfy the queries of individuals, especially about things
the knowledge of which men ought to obtain in all sin-
cerity, before God, for themselves, in humility by the
prayer of faith; and more especially a teacher or a high
priest in the Church. (*D.H.C.* I, 339)

Necessity of Revelation

The plea of many in this day is that we have no right
to receive revelations; but if we do not get revelations,
we do not have the oracles of God; and if they have not
the oracles of God, they are not the people of God. But
say you, What will become of the world, or the various
professors of religion who do not believe in revelation and
the oracles of God as continued to his Church in all ages
of the world, when he has a people on earth? I tell you,
in the name of Jesus Christ, they will be damned; and
when you get into the eternal world, you will find it will
be so; they cannot escape the damnation of hell. (*D.H.C.*
V, 257)

The Holy Ghost a Revelator

No man can receive the Holy Ghost without receiving
revelations. The Holy Ghost is a revelator. (*D.H.C.* VI,
58)

The Spirit of Revelation

The spirit of revelation is in connection with these
blessings. A person may profit by noticing the first intima-
tion of the spirit of revelation; for instance, when you feel
pure intelligence flowing into you, it may give you sudden
strokes of ideas, so that by noticing it, you may find it
fulfilled the same day or soon; (i.e.) those things that
were presented unto your minds by the Spirit of God,
will come to pass; and thus by learning the Spirit of God
and understanding it, you may grow into the principle

of revelation, until you become perfect in Christ Jesus.
(*D.H.C.* III, 381)

The Things of God Are of Deep Import

. . . the things of God are of deep import; and time,
and experience, and careful and ponderous and solemn
thoughts can only find them out. Thy mind, O man! if
thou wilt lead a soul unto salvation, must stretch as high
as the utmost heavens, and search into and contemplate
the darkest abyss, and the broad expanse of eternity—thou
must commune with God. How much more dignified and
noble are the thoughts of God, than the vain imaginations
of the human heart! (*D.H.C.* III, 295)

Revelation Is Given when the People Are Able to Receive It

"Some people say I am a fallen Prophet, because I
do not bring forth more of the word of the Lord. Why
did I not do it? Are we able to receive it? No! not one
in this room. He then chastened the congregation for their
wickedness and unbelief, 'for whom the Lord loveth he
chasteneth, and scourgeth every son and daughter whom
he receiveth,' and if we do not receive chastisements then
we are bastards and not sons."

On the subject of revelation, he said, a man would
command his son to dig potatoes and saddle his horse, but
before he had done either he would tell him to do something else. This is all considered right; but as soon as the
Lord gives a commandment and revokes that decree and
commands something else, then the Prophet is considered
fallen. (*D.H.C.* IV, 478)

Importance of Revelation

Salvation cannot come without revelation; it is in vain
for anyone to minister without it. No man is a minister
of Jesus Christ without being a prophet. No man can be

a minister of Jesus Christ except he has the testimony of Jesus; and this is the spirit of prophecy. Whenever salvation has been administered, it has been by testimony. Men of the present time testify of heaven and hell, and have never seen either; and I will say that no man knows these things without this. (*D.H.C.* III, 389-390)

Revelation and Obedience thereto Brings Blessings

. . . we cannot keep all the commandments without first knowing them, and we cannot expect to know all, or more than we now know unless we comply with or keep those we have already received. That which is wrong under one circumstance, may be, and often is, right under another.

God said, "Thou shalt not kill"; at another time he said "Thou shalt utterly destroy." This is the principle on which the government of heaven is conducted—by revelation adapted to the circumstances in which the children of the kingdom are placed. Whatever God requires is right, no matter what it is, although we may not see the reason thereof till long after the events transpire. If we seek first the kingdom of God, all good things will be added. So with Solomon: first he asked wisdom, and God gave it him, and with it every desire of his heart, even things which might be considered abominable to all who understand the order of heaven only in part, but which in reality were right because God gave and sanctioned by special revelation.

A parent may whip a child, and justly, too, because he stole an apple; whereas if the child had asked for the apple, and the parent had given it, the child would have eaten it with a better appetite; there would have been no stripes; all the pleasure of the apple would have been secured, all the misery of stealing lost.

This principle will justly apply to all of God's dealings with his children. Everything that God gives us is lawful and right; and it is proper that we should enjoy his gifts and blessings whenever and wherever he is disposed to bestow; but if we should seize upon those same blessings and enjoyments without law, without revelation, without commandment, those blessings and enjoyments would prove cursings and vexations in the end, and we should have to lie down in sorrow and wailings of everlasting regret. But in obedience there is joy and peace unspotted, unalloyed; and as God has designed our happiness—and the happiness of all his creatures, he never has—he never will institute an ordinance or give a commandment to his people that is not calculated in its nature to promote that happiness which he has designed, and which will not end in the greatest amount of good and glory to those who become the recipients of his law and ordinances. Blessings offered, but rejected, are no longer blessings, but become like the talent hid in the earth by the wicked and slothful servant; the proffered good returns to the giver; the blessing is bestowed on those who will receive and occupy; for unto him that hath shall be given, and he shall have abundantly, but unto him that hath not or will not receive, shall be taken away that which he hath, or might have had.

> Be wise today; 'tis madness to defer:
> Next day the fatal precedent may plead.
> Thus on till wisdom is pushed out of time
> Into eternity.

Our Heavenly Father is more liberal in his views, and boundless in his mercies and blessings, than we are ready to believe or receive; and, at the same time, is more terrible to the workers of iniquity, more awful in the executions of his punishments, and more ready to detect every false way, than we are apt to suppose him to be. He will be inquired of by his children. He says: "Ask and ye shall receive, seek and ye shall find"; (See Matt. 7:7) but, if you will take that which is not your own, or which I have not given you, you shall be rewarded according to your deeds; but no good thing will I withhold from them who walk uprightly before me, and do my will in all things—who will listen to my voice and to the voice of my servant whom I have sent; for I delight in those who seek diligently to know my precepts, and abide by the law of my kingdom; for all things shall be made known unto them in mine own due time, and in the end they shall have joy. (*D.H.C.* V, 135-136)

Powerful Discourses Are Preached by the Power of the Holy Priesthood and the Holy Ghost

When the Twelve or any other witnesses stand before the congregations of the earth, and they preach in the power and demonstration of the Spirit of God, and the people are astonished and confounded at the doctrine, and say, "That man has preached a powerful discourse, a great sermon," then let that man or those men take care that they do not ascribe the glory unto themselves, but be careful that they are humble, and ascribe the praise and glory to God and the Lamb; for it is by the power of the Holy Priesthood and the Holy Ghost that they have power thus to speak. (*D.H.C.* III, 384)

Revelation Not to Be Received for One of Higher Authority

I will inform you that it is contrary to the economy of God for any member of the Church, or anyone, to receive instruction for those in authority, higher than themselves; therefore you will see the impropriety of giving heed to them; but if any person have a vision or a visitation from a heavenly messenger, it must be for his own benefit and instruction; for the fundamental principles, government, and doctrine of the Church are vested in the keys of the kingdom. . . . (*D.H.C.* I, 338)

Principles of Astronomy Given to the Prophet

This afternoon I labored on the Egyptian alphabet, in company with Brothers Oliver Cowdery and W. W.

Phelps, and during the research, the principles of astronomy as understood by Father Abraham and the ancients unfolded to our understanding, the particulars of which will appear hereafter. (*D.H.C.* II, 286)

Revelation—The Order of Heavenly Things

. . . All men are liars who say they are of the true Church without the revelations of Jesus Christ and the priesthood of Melchizedek, which is after the order of the Son of God.

It is in the order of heavenly things that God should always send a new dispensation into the world when men have apostatized from the truth and lost the priesthood; but when men come out and build upon other men's foundations, they do it on their own responsibility, without authority from God; and when the floods come and the winds blow, their foundations will be found to be sand, and their whole fabric will crumble to dust.

Did I build on any other man's foundations? I have got all the truth which the Christian world possessed, and an independent revelation in the bargain, and God will bear me off triumphant. I will drop this subject. I wish I could speak for three or four hours; but it is not expedient on account of the rain: I would still go on, and show you proof upon proofs; all the Bible is equal in support of this doctrine, one part as another. (*D.H.C.* VI, 478-479)

Revelation Necessary

. . . I believe all that God ever revealed, and I never hear of a man being damned for believing too much; but they are damned for unbelief. (*D.H.C.* VI, 477)

Spiritual Discernment

. . . we came into a piece of thick woods of recent growth, where I told them that I felt much depressed in spirit and lonesome, and that there had been a great deal of bloodshed in that place, remarking that whenever a man of God is in a place where many have been killed, he will feel lonesome and unpleasant, and his spirits will sink. (*D.H.C.* II, 66)

God Reveals Himself to Men

. . . I was this morning introduced to a man from the east. After hearing my name, he remarked that I was nothing but a man, indicating by this expression, that he had supposed that a person to whom the Lord should see fit to reveal his will, must be something more than a man. He seemed to have forgotten the saying that fell from the lips of James, that Elias was a man subject to like passions as we are, yet he had such power with God, that he, in answer to his prayers, shut the heavens that they gave no rain for the space of three years and six months; and again, in answer to his prayer, the heavens gave forth rain, and the earth gave forth fruit. Indeed, such is the darkness and ignorance of this generation, that they look upon it as incredible that a man should have any intercourse with his Maker. (*D.H.C.* II, 302)

No Error in the Revelations

When did I ever teach anything wrong from this stand? When was I ever confounded? I want to triumph in Israel before I depart hence and am no more seen. I never told you I was perfect; but there is no error in the revelations which I have taught. . . . (*D.H.C.* VI, 366)

CHAPTER FOUR

The Kingdom of God

How to Identify the Kingdom of God

Whenever men can find out the will of God and find an administrator legally authorized from God, there is the kingdom of God; but where these are not, the kingdom of God is not. All the ordinances, systems, and administrations on the earth are of no use to the children of men, unless they are ordained and authorized of God; for nothing will save a man but a legal administrator; for none others will be acknowledged either by God or angels. (*D.H.C.* V, 259)

What Constitutes the Kingdom of God

Some say the kingdom of God was not set up on the earth until the Day of Pentecost, and that John did not preach the baptism of repentance for the remission of sins; but I say, in the name of the Lord, that the kingdom of God was set up on the earth from the days of Adam to the present time. Whenever there has been a righteous man on earth unto whom God revealed his word and gave power and authority to administer in his name, and where there is a priest of God—a minister who has power and authority from God to administer in the ordinances of the gospel and officiate in the priesthood of God, there is the kingdom of God; and, in consequence of rejecting the Gospel of Jesus Christ and the prophets whom God hath sent, the judgments of God have rested upon people, cities, and nations, in various ages of the world, which was the case with the cities of Sodom and Gomorrah, that were destroyed for rejecting the prophets.

Now I will give my testimony. I care not for man. I speak boldly and faithfully and with authority. How is it with the kingdom of God? Where did the kingdom of God begin? Where there is no kingdom of God there is no salvation. What constitutes the kingdom of God? Where there is a prophet, a priest, or a righteous man unto whom God gives his oracles, there is the kingdom of God; and where the oracles of God are not, there the kingdom of God is not.

In these remarks, I have no allusion to the kingdoms of the earth. We will keep the laws of the land; we do not speak against them; we never have, and we can hardly make mention of the state of Missouri, of our persecutions there, etc., but what the cry goes forth that we are guilty of larceny, burglary, arson, treason, murder, etc., etc., which is false. We speak of the kingdom of God on the earth, not the kingdoms of men. (*D.H.C.* V, 256-257)

The Kingdom of God

But, says one, the kingdom of God could not be set up in the days of John, for John said the kingdom was at hand. But I would ask if it could be any nearer to them than to be in the hands of John. The people need not wait for the days of Pentecost to find the kingdom of God, for John had it with him, and he came forth from the wilderness crying out, "Repent ye, for the kingdom of heaven is nigh at hand," as much as to say, "Out here I have got the kingdom of God and I am coming after you; I have got the kingdom of God, and you can get it, and I am coming after you; and if you don't receive it, you will be damned"; and the scriptures represent that all Jerusalem went out unto John's baptism. There was a legal administrator, and those that were baptized were subjects for a king; and also the laws and oracles of God were there; therefore the kingdom of God was there; for no man could have better authority to administer than John; and our Savior submitted to that authority himself, by being baptized by

John; therefore the kingdom of God was set up on the earth, even in the days of John.

There is a difference between the kingdom of God and the fruits and blessings that flow from the kingdom; because there were more miracles, gifts, visions, healings, tongues, etc., in the days of Jesus Christ and his apostles, and on the Day of Pentecost, than under John's administration, it does not prove by any means that John had not the kingdom of God, any more than it would that a woman had not a milkpan because she had not a pan of milk, for while the pan might be compared to the kingdom, the milk might be compared to the blessings of the kingdom. (*D.H.C.* V, 257-258)

Seeing or Entering into the Kingdom of God

It is one thing to see the kingdom of God, and another thing to enter into it. We must have a change of heart to see the kingdom of God, and subscribe the articles of adoption to enter therein. (*D.H.C.* VI, 58)

God's Kingdom Never to Be Destroyed

. . . The ancient prophets declared that in the last days the God of heaven should set up a kingdom which should never be destroyed, nor left to other people; and the very time that was calculated on, this people were struggling to bring it out. (*D.H.C.* VI, 364)

The Kingdom of God and the Kingdom of the Devil

. . . In relation to the kingdom of God, the devil always set up his kingdom at the very same time in opposition to God. (*D.H.C.* VI, 364)

How the Kingdom of God Will Roll On

I calculate to be one of the instruments of setting up the kingdom of Daniel by the word of the Lord, and I intend to lay a foundation that will revolutionize the whole world. I once offered my life to the Missouri mob as a sacrifice for my people, and here I am. It will not be by sword or gun that this kingdom will roll on: the power of truth is such that all nations will be under the necessity of obeying the Gospel. The prediction is that army will be against army: it may be that the Saints will have to beat their ploughs into swords, for it will not do for men to sit down patiently and see their children destroyed. (*D.H.C.* VI, 365)

CHAPTER FIVE

First Principles of the Gospel and Gifts of the Spirit

Eternal Judgments and First Principles

The doctrine of eternal judgments belongs to the first principles of the Gospel, in the last days. (*D.H.C.* VI, 364)

Faith, Repentance, Baptism, and the Holy Ghost

Faith comes by hearing the word of God, through the testimony of the servants of God; that testimony is always attended by the Spirit of prophecy and revelation.

Repentance is a thing that cannot be trifled with every day. Daily transgression and daily repentance is not that which is pleasing in the sight of God.

Baptism is a holy ordinance preparatory to the reception of the Holy Ghost; it is the channel and key by which the Holy Ghost will be administered.

The gift of the Holy Ghost by the laying on of hands, cannot be received through the medium of any other principle than the principle of righteousness, for if the proposals are not complied with, it is of no use, but withdraws. (*D.H.C.* III, 379)

Faith

Because faith is wanting, the fruits are. No man since the world has had faith without having something along with it. The ancients quenched the violence of fire, escaped the edge of the sword, women received their dead, etc. By faith the worlds were made. A man who has none of the gifts has no faith; and he deceives himself, if he supposes he has. Faith has been wanting, not only among the heathen, but in professed Christendom also, so that tongues, healings, prophecy, and prophets and apostles, and all the gifts and blessings have been wanting. (*D.H.C.* V, 218)

Faith and Its Fruits

. . . Faith comes by hearing the word of God. If a man has not faith enough to do one thing, he may have faith to do another; if he cannot remove a mountain, he may heal the sick. Where faith is, there will be some of the fruits: all gifts and power which were sent from heaven, were poured out on the heads of those who had faith. (*D.H.C.* V, 355)

Exercising Great Faith Causes Physical Weakness

Elder Jedediah M. Grant inquired of me the cause of my turning pale and losing strength last night while blessing children. I told him that I saw that Lucifer would exert his influence to destroy the children that I was blessing, and I strove with all the faith and spirit that I had to seal upon them a blessing that would secure their lives upon the earth; and so much virtue went out of me into the children, that I became weak, from which I have not yet recovered; and I referred to the case of the woman touching the hem of the garment of Jesus. (Luke 8) The virtue here referred to is the spirit of life; and a man who exercises great faith in administering to the sick, blessing little children, or confirming, is liable to become weakened. (*D.H.C.* V, 303)

Repentance and Forgiveness

. . . How glorious are the principles of righteousness! We are full of selfishness; the devil flatters us that we are very righteous when we are feeding on the faults of others. We can only live by worshiping our God; all must do it for themselves; none can do it for another. How mild the Savior dealt with Peter, saying, "When thou art converted, strengthen thy brethren." At another time, he said to him, "Lovest thou me?" and having received Peter's reply, he said, "Feed my sheep." If the sisters loved the Lord, let them feed the sheep, and not destroy them. How oft have wise men and women sought to dictate Brother Joseph by saying, "O, if I were Brother Joseph, I would do this and that"; but if they were in Brother Joseph's shoes they would find that men or women could not be compelled into the kingdom of God, but must be dealt with in long-suffering, and at last we shall save them. The way to keep all the Saints together, and keep the work rolling, is to wait with all long-suffering, till God shall bring such characters to justice. There should be no license for sin, but mercy should go hand in hand with reproof.

Sisters of the society, shall there be strife among you? I will not have it. You must repent, and get the love of God. Away with self-righteousness. The best measure or principles to bring the poor to repentance is to administer to their wants. The Ladies' Relief Society is not only to relieve the poor, but to save souls. (*D.H.C.* V, 24-25)

The Principles of Mercy, Repentance and Forgiveness

. . . said he was going to preach mercy. Suppose that Jesus Christ and holy angels should object to us on frivolous things, what would become of us? We must be merciful to one another, and overlook small things.

. . . It grieves me that there is no fuller fellowship; if one member suffer all feel it; by union of feeling we obtain power with God. Christ said he came to call sinners to repentance, to save them. Christ was condemned by the self-righteous Jews because he took sinners into his society; he took them upon the principle that they repented of their sins. It is the object of this society [he was speaking to the Relief Society] to reform persons, not to take those that are corrupt and foster them in their wickedness; but if they repent, we are bound to take them, and by kindness sanctify and cleanse them from all unrighteousness by our influence in watching over them. Nothing will have such influence over people as the fear of being disfellowshiped by so goodly a society as this. . . .

Nothing is so much calculated to lead people to forsake sin as to take them by the hand, and watch over them with tenderness. When persons manifest the least kindness and love to me, O what power it has over my mind, while the opposite course has a tendency to harrow up all the harsh feelings and depress the human mind.

It is one evidence that men are unacquainted with the principles of godliness to behold the contraction of affectionate feelings and lack of charity in the world. The power and glory of godliness is spread out on a broad principle to throw out the mantle of charity. God does not look on sin with allowance, but when men have sinned, there must be allowance made for them.

All the religious world is boasting of righteousness: it is the doctrine of the devil to retard the human mind, and hinder our progress, by filling us with self-righteousness. The nearer we get to our Heavenly Father, the more we are disposed to look with compassion on perishing souls; we feel that we want to take them upon our shoulders, and cast their sins behind our backs. My talk is intended for all this [Relief] society; if you would have God have mercy on you, have mercy on one another. (*D.H.C.* V, 23-24)

The Spirit of Forgiveness

There is another error which opens a door for the adversary to enter. As females possess refined feelings and sensitiveness, they are also subject to overmuch zeal, which must ever prove dangerous, and cause them to be rigid in a religious capacity—[they] should be armed with mercy, notwithstanding the iniquity among us.

Said he had been instrumental in bringing iniquity to light—it was a melancholy thought and awful that so many should place themselves under the condemnation of the devil, and going to perdition. With deep feeling he said that they are fellow mortals, we loved them once, shall we not encourage them to reformation? We have not [yet] forgiven them seventy times seven, as our Savior directed; perhaps we have not forgiven them once. There is now a day of salvation to such as repent and reform;—and they who repent not should be cast out from this society; yet we should woo them to return to God, lest they escape not the damnation of hell! Where there is a mountaintop, there is also a valley—we should act in all things on a proper medium to every immortal spirit. Notwithstanding the unworthy are among us, the virtuous should not, from self-importance, grieve and oppress needlessly, those unfortunate ones—even these should be encouraged hereafter to live to be honored by this society, who are the best portions of the community. Said he had two things to recommend to the members of this society, to put a double watch over the tongue: no organized body can exist without this at all. All organized bodies have their peculiar evils, weaknesses and difficulties, the object is to make those not so good reform and return to the path of virtue that they may be numbered with the good, and even hold the keys of power, which will influence to virtue and goodness—should chasten and reprove, and keep it all in silence, not even mention them again; then you will be established in power, virtue, and holiness, and the wrath of God will be turned away. (D.H.C. V, 19-20)

Forgiveness

Ever keep in exercise the principle of mercy, and be ready to forgive our brother on the first intimations of repentance, and asking forgiveness; and should we even forgive our brother, or even our enemy, before he repent or ask forgiveness, our Heavenly Father would be equally as merciful unto us. (*D.H.C.* III, 383)

How God Judges Mankind

. . . God judges men according to the use they make of the light which he gives them. (*D.H.C.* V, 401)

Baptism Necessary for Entrance into the Celestial Kingdom

Every man lives for himself. Adam was made to open the way of the world, and for dressing the garden. Noah was born to save seed of everything when the earth was washed of its wickedness by the flood; and the Son of God came into the world to redeem it from the fall. But except a man be born again, he cannot see the kingdom of God. This eternal truth settles the question of all men's religion. A man may be saved, after the judgment, in the terrestrial kingdom, or in the telestial kingdom, but he can never see the celestial kingdom of God, without being born of water and the Spirit. He may receive a glory like unto the moon, (i.e. of which the light of the moon is typical), or a star, (i.e. of which the light of the stars is typical), but he can never come unto Mount Zion, and unto the city of the living God, the heavenly Jerusalem, and to an innumerable company of angels; to the general assembly and Church of the Firstborn, which are written in heaven, and to God the judge of all, and to the spirits of just men made perfect, and to Jesus the Mediator of the new covenant, unless he becomes as a little child, and is taught by the Spirit of God. . . . (*D.H.C.* I, 283)

Infant Baptism False Doctrine

The doctrine of baptizing children, or sprinkling them, or they must welter in hell, is a doctrine not true, not supported in Holy Writ, and is not consistent with the character of God. All children are redeemed by the blood of Jesus Christ, and the moment that children leave this world, they are taken to the bosom of Abraham. (*D.H.C.* IV, 554)

Infant Baptism Not Necessary

"Do you believe in the baptism of infants?" asks the Presbyterian. No. "Why?" Because it is nowhere written in the Bible. Circumcision is not baptism, neither was baptism instituted in the place of circumcision. Baptism is for remission of sins. Children have no sins. Jesus blessed them and said, "Do what you have seen me do." Children are all made alive in Christ, and those of riper years through faith and repentance. (*D.H.C.* V, 499)

Re-entering the Church

. . . Respecting an apostate, or one who has been cut off from the Church, and who wishes to come in again, the law of our Church expressly says that such shall repent, and be baptized, and be admitted as at the first. (*D.H.C.* I, 338)

Baptism a Sign Ordained of God

. . . God has set many signs on the earth, as well as in the heavens; for instance, the oak of the forest, the fruit of the tree, the herb of the field—all bear a sign that seed hath been planted there; for it is a decree of the Lord that every tree, plant, and herb-bearing seed should bring forth of its kind, and cannot come forth after any other law or principle. Upon the same principle do I contend that baptism is a sign ordained of God, for the believer in Christ to take upon himself in order to enter into the kingdom of God, "for except ye are born of water and of the Spirit ye cannot enter into the kingdom of God," said the Savior. It is a sign and a commandment which God has set for man to enter into his kingdom. Those who seek to enter in any other way will seek in vain; for God will not receive them, neither will the angels acknowledge their works as accepted, for they have not obeyed the ordinances, nor attended to the signs which God ordained for the salvation of man, to prepare him for, and give him a title to, a celestial glory; and God had decreed that all who will not obey his voice shall not escape the damnation of hell. What is the damnation of hell? To go with that society who have not obeyed his commands.

Baptism is a sign to God, to angels, and to heaven that we do the will of God, and there is no other way beneath the heavens whereby God hath ordained for man to come to him to be saved, and enter into the kingdom of God, except faith in Jesus Christ, repentance, and baptism for the remission of sins, and any other course is in vain; then you have the promise of the gift of the Holy Ghost. (*D.H.C.* IV, 554-555)

Baptism

. . . The baptism of water, without the baptism of fire and the Holy Ghost attending it, is of no use; they are necessarily and inseparably connected. An individual must be born of water and of the spirit in order to get into the kingdom of God. In the German, the text bears me out the same as the revelations which I have given and taught for the past fourteen years on that subject. I have the testimony to put in their teeth. My testimony has been true all the time. You will find it in the declaration of John the Baptist. (Reads from the German.) John says, "I baptize you with water, but when Jesus comes, who has the power (or keys) he shall administer the baptism of fire and the Holy Ghost." Great God! Where is now all the sectarian world? And if this testimony is true, they are all damned as clearly as anathema can do it. I know the text is true. I call upon all you Germans who know that it is true to say, Aye. (Loud shouts of "Aye.")

Alexander Campbell, how are you going to save people with water alone? For John said his baptism was good for nothing without the baptism of Jesus Christ. "Therefore, *not* leaving the principles of the doctrine of Christ, let us go on unto perfection; not laying again the foundation of repentance from dead works, and of faith towards God, of the doctrine of baptism, and of laying on of hands, and of resurrection of the dead, and of eternal judgment. And this will we do, if God permit." (Heb. 6:1-3)

There is one God, one Father, one Jesus, one hope of our calling, one baptism. All these three baptisms only make one. Many talk of baptism not being essential to salvation; but this kind of teaching would lay the foundation of their damnation. I have the truth, and am at the defiance of the world to contradict me, if they can. (*D.H.C.* VI, 316-317)

Baptism and the Holy Ghost

. . . The gospel requires baptism by immersion for the remission of sins, which is the meaning of the word in the original language—namely, to bury or immerse.

We ask the sects, Do you believe this? They answer, No. I believe in being converted. I believe in this tenaciously. So did the Apostle Peter and the disciples of Jesus. But I further believe in the gift of the Holy Ghost by the laying on of hands. Evidence by Peter's preaching on the Day of Pentecost. (Acts 2:38) You might as well baptize a bag of sand as a man, if not done in view of the remission of sins and getting of the Holy Ghost. Baptism by water is but half a baptism, and is good for nothing without the other half—that is, the baptism of the Holy Ghost.

The Savior says, "Except a man be born of water and of the Spirit, he cannot enter into the kingdom of God." "Though we or an angel from heaven, preach any other gospel unto you than that which we have preached unto you, let him be accursed," according to Galatians 1:8. (*D.H.C.* V, 499-500)

The Holy Ghost Comes in the Sign of the Dove

... Whoever led the Son of God into the waters of baptism, and had the privilege of beholding the Holy Ghost descend in the form of a dove, or rather in the *sign* of the dove, in witness of that administration? The sign of the dove was instituted before the creation of the world, a witness for the Holy Ghost, and the devil cannot come in the sign of a dove. The Holy Ghost is a personage, and is in the form of a personage. It does not confine itself to the *form* of the dove, but in *sign* of the dove. The Holy Ghost cannot be transformed into a dove; but the sign of a dove was given to John to signify the truth of the deed, as the dove is an emblem or token of truth and innocence. (*D.H.C.* V, 260-261)

Speaking in Tongues Not to be Sought After

Be not so curious about tongues; do not speak in tongues except there be an interpreter present; the ultimate design of tongues is to speak to foreigners, and if persons are very anxious to display their intelligence, let them speak to such in their own tongues. The gifts of God are all useful in their place, but when they are applied to that which God does not intend, they prove an injury, a snare and a curse instead of a blessing. We may some future time enter more fully into this subject, but shall let this suffice for the present. (*D.H.C.* V, 31-32)

Greatest Gifts of God Not Known by an Observer

The greatest, the best, and the most useful gifts would be known nothing about by an observer. It is true that a man might prophesy, which is a great gift, and one that Paul told the people—the Church—to seek after and to covet, rather than to speak in tongues; but what does the world know about prophesying? Paul says that it "serveth only to those that believe." But do not the scriptures say that they spake in tongues and prophesied? Yes; but who is it that writes these scriptures? Not the men of the world or mere casual observers, but the apostles—men who knew one gift from another, and of course were capable of writing about it; if we had the testimony of the scribes and Pharisees concerning the outpouring of the Spirit on the Day of Pentecost, they would have told us that it was no gift, but that the people were "drunken with new wine," and we shall finally have to come to the same conclusion that Paul did—"No man knows the things of God but by the Spirit of God"; for with the great revelations of Paul when he was caught up into the third heaven and saw things that were not lawful to utter, no man was apprised of it until he mentioned it himself fourteen years after; and when John had the curtains of heaven withdrawn, and by vision looked through the dark vista of future ages, and contemplated events that should transpire throughout every subsequent period of time, until the final winding up scene—while he gazed upon the glories of the eternal world, saw an innumerable company of angels and heard the voice of God—it was in the Spirit, on the Lord's day, unnoticed and unobserved by the world.

The manifestations of the gift of the Holy Ghost, the ministering of angels, or the development of the power, majesty or glory of God were very seldom manifested publicly, and that generally to the people of God, as to the Israelites; but most generally when angels have come, or God has revealed himself, it has been to individuals in private, in their chamber; in the wilderness or fields, and that generally without noise or tumult. The angel delivered Peter out of prison in the dead of night; came to Paul unobserved by the rest of the crew; appeared to Mary and Elizabeth without the knowledge of others; spoke to John the Baptist whilst the people around were ignorant of it.

When Elisha saw the chariots of Israel and the horsemen thereof, it was unknown to others. When the Lord appeared to Abraham it was at his tent door; when the

angels went to Lot, no person knew them but himself,
which was the case probably with Abraham and his wife;
when the Lord appeared to Moses, it was in the burning
bush, in the tabernacle, or on the mountaintop; when
Elijah was taken in a chariot of fire, it was unobserved by
the world; and when he was in a cleft of a rock, there was
loud thunder, but the Lord was not in the thunder; there
was an earthquake, but the Lord was not in the earthquake; and then there was a still small voice, which was
the voice of the Lord, saying, "What doest thou hear,
Elijah?"

The Lord cannot always be known by the thunder of
his voice, by the display of his glory or by the manifestation of his power; and those that are the most anxious to
see these things, are the least prepared to meet them, and
were the Lord to manifest his power as he did to the children of Israel, such characters would be the first to say,
"Let not the Lord speak any more, lest we his people die."
(*D.H.C.* V, 30-31)

Gifts of the Spirit

. . . Paul says, "To one is given the gift of tongues,
to another the gift of prophecy, and to another the gift
of healing"; and again: "Do all prophesy? do all speak
with tongues? do all interpret?" evidently showing that all
did not possess these several gifts; but that one received
one gift, and another received another gift—all did not
prophesy, all did not speak in tongues, all did not work
miracles; but all did receive the gift of the Holy Ghost;
sometimes they spake in tongues and prophesied in the
apostles' days, and sometimes they did not. The same is
the case with us also in our administrations, while more
frequently there is no manifestation at all that is visible
to the surrounding multitude; this will appear plain when
we consult the writings of the apostles, and notice their
proceedings in relation to this matter. Paul said, "Now
concerning spiritual gifts, brethren, I would not have you

ignorant"; (I Cor. 12:1) it is evident from this, that some of them were ignorant in relation to these matters, or they would not need instruction.

Again in chapter xiv, he says, "Follow after charity, and desire spiritual gifts, but rather that ye may prophesy." (*Ibid.*, 14:1) It is very evident from these scriptures that many of them had not spiritual gifts, for if they had spiritual gifts where was the necessity of Paul telling them to follow after them, and it is as evident that they did not all receive those gifts by the imposition of the hands; for they as a Church had been baptized and confirmed by the laying on of hands—and yet to a Church of this kind under the immediate inspection and superintendency of the apostles, it was necessary for Paul to say, "Follow after charity, and desire spiritual gifts, but rather that ye may prophesy," evidently showing that those gifts were in the Church, but not enjoyed by all in their outward manifestations.

But suppose the gifts of the Spirit were immediately, upon the imposition of hands, enjoyed by all, in all their fulness and power; the skeptic would still be as far from receiving any testimony except upon a mere casualty as before, for all the gifts of the Spirit are not visible to the natural vision, or understanding of man; indeed very few of them are. We read that "Christ ascended into heaven and gave gifts unto men; and he gave some apostles, and some prophets, and some evangelists, and some pastors and teachers." (See Eph. 4:11.)

The Church is a compact body composed of different members, and is strictly analogous to the human system, and Paul, after speaking of the different gifts, said, "Now ye are the body of Christ and members in particular; and God hath set some in the Church, first apostles, secondarily prophets, thirdly teachers, after that miracles, then gifts of healing, helps, governments, diversities of tongues. Are all teachers? Are all workers of miracles? Do all speak with tongues? Do all interpret?" It is evident that they do not; yet are they all members of one body. All members of the natural body are not the eye, the ear, the head or the hand—". . . the eye cannot say to the ear I have no need of thee, nor the head to the foot, I have no need of thee"; (See I Cor. 12:12-22.) they are all so many component parts in the perfect machine—the one body; and if one member suffer, the whole of the members suffer with it; and if one member rejoice, all the rest are honored with it.

These, then, are all gifts; they come from God; they are of God; they are all the gifts of the Holy Ghost; they are what Christ ascended into heaven to impart; and yet how few of them could be known by the generality of men. Peter and John were apostles, yet the Jewish court scourged them as impostors. Paul was both an apostle and prophet, yet they stoned him and put him into prison. The people knew nothing about it, although he had in his possession the gift of the Holy Ghost. Our Savior was "anointed with the oil of gladness above his fellows," yet so far from the people knowing him, they said he was Beelzebub, and crucified him as an impostor. Who could point out a pastor, a teacher, or an evangelist by their appearance, yet had they the gift of the Holy Ghost?

But to come to the other members of the Church, and examine the gifts as spoken of by Paul, and we shall find that the world can in general know nothing about them, and that there is but one or two that could be immediately known, if they were all poured out immediately upon the imposition of hands. Paul said, "There are diversities of gifts yet the same Spirit, and there are differences of administrations, but the same Lord; And there are diversities of operations, but it is the same God which worketh all in all. But the manifestation of the Spirit is given unto every man to profit withal. For to one is given, by the Spirit the word of wisdom; to another the word of knowledge by the same Spirit; To another faith by the same Spirit; to another the gifts of healing, by the same Spirit; To another the working of miracles; to another prophecy; to another the discerning of spirits; to another divers kinds of tongues; to another the interpretation of tongues. But all these worketh that one and the self same Spirit, dividing to each man severally as he will." (I Cor. 12:4-11)

There are several gifts mentioned here, yet which of them all could be known by an observer at the imposition of hands? The word of wisdom, and the word of knowledge, are as much gifts as any other, yet if a person possessed both of these gifts, or received them by the imposition of hands, who would know it? Another might receive the gift of faith, and they would be as ignorant of it. Or suppose a man had the gift of healing or power to work miracles, that would not then be known; it would require time and circumstances to call these gifts into operation. Suppose a man had the discerning of spirits, who would be the wiser for it? Or if he had the interpretation of tongues, unless someone spoke in an unknown tongue, he of course would have to be silent; there are only two gifts that could be made visible—the gift of tongues and the gift of prophecy. These are things that are the most talked about, and yet if a person spoke in an unknown tongue, according to Paul's testimony, he would be a barbarian to those present. They would say that it was gibberish; and if he prophesied they would call it nonsense. The gift of tongues is the smallest gift perhaps of the whole, and yet it is one that is the most sought after. (D.H.C. V, 28-30)

The Gift of the Holy Ghost

Various and conflicting are the opinions of men in regard to the gift of the Holy Ghost. Some people have been in the habit of calling every supernatural manifestation the effects of the Spirit of God, whilst there are others that think there is no manifestation connected with it at all; and that it is nothing but a mere impulse of the mind, or an inward feeling, impression, or secret testimony or evidence, which men possess, and that there is no such a thing as an outward manifestation.

It is not to be wondered at that men should be ignorant, in a great measure, of the principles of salvation, and more especially of the nature, office, power, influence, gifts, and blessings of the gift of the Holy Ghost; when we consider that the human family have been enveloped in gross darkness and ignorance for many centuries past, without revelation, or any just criterion [by which] to arrive at a knowledge of the things of God, which can only be known by the Spirit of God. Hence it not infrequently occurs, that when the elders of this Church preach to the inhabitants of the world, that if they obey the Gospel they shall receive the gift of the Holy Ghost, that the people expect to see some wonderful manifestation, some great display of power, or some extraordinary miracle performed; and it is often the case that young members of this Church, for want of better information, carry along with them their old notions of things, and sometimes fall into egregious errors. We have lately had some information concerning a few members that are in this dilemma, and for their information make a few remarks upon the subject.

We believe in the gift of the Holy Ghost being enjoyed now, as much as it was in the apostles' days; we believe that it [the gift of the Holy Ghost] is necessary to make and to organize the priesthood, that no man can be called to fill any office in the ministry without it; we also believe in prophecy, in tongues, in visions, and in revelations, in gifts, and in healings; and that these things cannot be enjoyed without the gift of the Holy Ghost. We believe that the holy men of old spake as they were moved by the Holy Ghost, and that holy men in these days speak by the same principle; we believe in its being a comforter and a witness bearer, that it brings things past to our remembrance, leads us into all truth, and shows us of things to come; we believe that "no man can know

that Jesus is the Christ, but by the Holy Ghost." We believe in it [this gift of the Holy Ghost] in all its fulness,
and power, and greatness, and glory; but whilst we do
this, we believe in it rationally, consistently, and scriptur-
ally, and not according to the wild vagaries, foolish notions
and traditions of men.

The human family are very apt to run to extremes,
especially in religious matters, and hence people in general, either want some miraculous display, or they will not
believe in the gift of the Holy Ghost at all. If an elder
lays his hands upon a person, it is thought by many that
the person must immediately rise and speak in tongues
and prophesy; this idea is gathered from the circumstance
of Paul laying his hands upon certain individuals who had
been previously [as they stated] baptized unto John's
baptism; which when he had done, they "spake in tongues
and prophesied." Philip also, when he had preached the
Gospel to the inhabitants of the city of Samaria, sent for
Peter and John, who when they came laid their hands
upon them for the gift of the Holy Ghost; for as yet he
was fallen upon none of them; and when Simon Magus
saw that through the laying on of the apostles' hands the
Holy Ghost was given, he offered them money that he
might possess the same power. (Acts 8) These pas-
sages are considered by many as affording sufficient evidence for some miraculous, visible manifestation, whenever
hands are laid on for the gift of the Holy Ghost.

We believe that the Holy Ghost is imparted by the
laying on of hands of those in authority, and that the gift
of tongues, and also the gift of prophecy are gifts of the
Spirit, and are obtained through that medium; but then
to say that men always prophesied and spoke in tongues
when they had the imposition of hands, would be to state
that which is untrue, contrary to the practice of the
apostles, and at variance with holy writ; . . . (*D.H.C.* V,
26-28)

The Gift of Tongues

Tongues were given for the purpose of preaching among those whose language is not understood; as on the Day of Pentecost, etc., and it is not necessary for tongues to be taught to the Church particularly, for any man that has the Holy Ghost, can speak of the things of God in his own tongue as well as to speak in another; for faith comes not by signs, but by hearing the word of God. (*D.H.C.* III, 379)

Difference between the Holy Ghost and the Gift of the Holy Ghost

There is a difference between the Holy Ghost and the gift of the Holy Ghost. Cornelius received the Holy Ghost before he was baptized, which was the convincing power of God unto him of the truth of the Gospel, but he could not receive the gift of the Holy Ghost until after he was baptized. Had he not taken this sign or ordinance upon him, the Holy Ghost which convinced him of the truth of God, would have left him. (*D.H.C.* IV, 555)

Gift of Tongues

The public meeting of the Saints was at my house this evening, and after Patriarch Hyrum Smith and Elder Brigham Young had spoken on the principles of faith, and the gifts of the Spirit, I read the 13th chapter of First Corinthians, also a part of the 14th chapter, and remarked that the gift of tongues was necessary in the Church; but that if Satan could not speak in tongues, he could not tempt a Dutchman, or any other nation, but the English, for he can tempt the Englishman, for he has tempted me, and I am an Englishman; but the gift of tongues by the power of the Holy Ghost in the Church is for the benefit of the servants of God to preach to unbelievers, as on the Day of Pentecost. When devout men from every nation shall assemble to hear the things of God, let the elders preach to them in their own mother tongue, whether it is German, French, Spanish or "Irish," or any other, and let those interpret who understand the language spoken, in their own mother tongue, and this is what the apostle meant in First Corinthians 14:27. (*D.H.C.* IV, 485-486)

The Gift of the Holy Ghost a Distinguishing Feature of the Church

In our interview with the President, [Van Buren] he interrogated us wherein we differed in our religion from the other religions of the day. Brother Joseph said we differed in mode of baptism, and the gift of the Holy Ghost by the laying on of hands. We considered that all other considerations were contained in the gift of the Holy Ghost, and we deemed it unnecessary to make many words in preaching the Gospel to him. Suffice it to say he has got our testimony. (*D.H.C.* IV, 42)

Gift of Tongues

. . . the gift of tongues is so often made use of by Satan to deceive the Saints. (*D.H.C.* II, 141)

The Gift of Tongues

. . . As to the gift of tongues, all we can say is, that in this place we have received it as the ancients did; we wish you, however, to be careful, lest in this you be deceived. Guard against evils which may arise from any accounts given by women, or otherwise; be careful in all things lest any root of bitterness spring up among you, and thereby many be defiled. Satan will no doubt trouble you about the gift of tongues, unless you are careful; you cannot watch him too closely, nor pray too much. May the Lord give you wisdom in all things. (*D.H.C.* I, 369)

Knowledge of God Comes by the Holy Ghost

President Smith arose and called the attention of the meeting to the 12th chapter 1st Corinthians—"Now concerning spiritual gifts, I would not have you ignorant." Said that the passage in the third verse, which reads, "no man can say that Jesus is the Lord, but by the Holy Ghost," should be translated "no man can *know* that Jesus is the Lord, but by the Holy Ghost." (*D.H.C.* IV, 602-603)

CHAPTER SIX

Missionary Work

Greatest and Most Important Duty of the Church

. . . After all that has been said, the greatest and most important duty is to preach the Gospel. (*D.H.C.* II, 478)

Responsibility of Missionaries to Preach Jesus Christ

. . . preach Jesus Christ and him crucified; not to contend with others on account of their faith, or systems of religion, but pursue a steady course. This I delivered by way of commandment; and all who observe it not, will pull down persecution upon their heads, while those who do, shall always be filled with the Holy Ghost; this I pronounced as a prophecy, and sealed with hosanna and amen. (*D.H.C.* II, 431)

Elders to Preach Repentance

Oh, ye elders of Israel, harken to my voice; and when you are sent into the world to preach, tell those things you are sent to tell; preach and cry aloud, "Repent ye, for the kingdom of heaven is at hand; repent and believe the Gospel." Declare the first principles, and let mysteries alone, lest ye be overthrown. Never meddle with the visions of beasts and subjects you do not understand. Elder Brown, when you go to Palmyra, say nothing about the four beasts, but preach those things the Lord has told you to preach about—repentance and baptism for the remission of sins. (*D.H.C.* V, 344)

The Mission Field Is the World

Take Jacob Zundell and Frederick H. Moeser, and tell them never to drink a drop of ale, wine, or any spirit, only that which flows right out from the presence of God; and send them to Germany; and when you meet with an Arab, send him to Arabia; when you find an Italian, send him to Italy; and a Frenchman, to France; or an Indian, that is suitable, send him among the Indians. Send them to the different places where they belong. Send somebody to Central America and to all Spanish America; and don't let a single corner of the earth go without a mission. (*D.H.C.* V, 368)

Salvation of Souls—A Paramount Responsibility of the Elders of the Church

. . . Every elder that can, after providing for his family (if he has any) and paying his debts, must go forth and clear his skirts from the blood of this generation. While they are in that region instead of trying members for transgressions, or offenses, let everyone labor to prepare himself for the vineyard, sparing a litle time to comfort the mourners; to bind up the brokenhearted; to reclaim the backslider; to bring back the wanderer; to reinvite into the kingdom such as have been cut off, by encouraging them to lay to while the day lasts, and work righteousness, and, with one heart and one mind, prepare to help redeem Zion, that goodly land of promise, where the willing and the obedient shall be blessed. Souls are as precious in the sight of God as they ever were; and the elders were never called to drive any down to hell, but to persuade and invite all men everywhere to repent, that they become the heirs of salvation. . . . Seek to help save souls, not to destroy them: for verily you know, that "there is more joy in heaven, over one sinner that repents, than there is over ninety and nine just persons that need no repentance." Strive not about the mysteries of the kingdom; cast not your pearls before swine, give not the bread of the children to dogs, lest you and the children should suffer, and you thereby offend your righteous Judge. (*D.H.C.* II, footnote pp. 229, 230)

Duties of Missionaries

And first, it becomes an elder when he is traveling through the world, warning the inhabitants of the earth to gather together, that there may be built up an holy city unto the Lord, instead of commencing with children, or those who look up to parents or guardians to influence their minds, thereby drawing them from their duties, which they rightfully owe these legal guardians, they should commence their labors with parents, or guardians; and their teachings should be such as are calculated to turn the hearts of the fathers to the children, and the hearts of children to the fathers; and no influence should be used with children, contrary to the consent of their parents or guardians; but all such as can be persuaded in a lawful and righteous manner, and with common consent, we should feel it our duty to influence them to gather with the people of God. But otherwise let the responsibility rest upon the heads of parents or guardians, and all condemnation or consequences be upon their heads, according to the dispensation which he hath committed unto us; for God hath so ordained, that his work shall be cut short in righteousness, in the last days; therefore, first teach the parents, and then, with their consent, persuade the children to embrace the Gospel also. And if children embrace the Gospel, and their parents or guardians are unbelievers, teach them to stay at home and be obedient to their parents or guardians, if they require it; but if they consent to let them gather with the people of God, let them do so, and there shall be no wrong; and let all things be done carefully and righteously and God will extend to all such his guardian care.

And secondly, it is the duty of elders, when they enter into any house, to let their labors and warning voice be unto the master of that house; and if he receive the Gospel, then he may extend his influence to his wife also, with consent, that peradventure she may receive the Gospel; but if a man receive not the Gospel, but gives his consent that his wife may receive it, and she believes, then let her receive it. But if a man forbid his wife, or his children, before they are of age, to receive the Gospel, then it should be the duty of the elder to go his way, and use no influence against him, and let the responsibility be upon his head; shake off the dust of thy feet as a testimony against him, and thy skirts shall then be clear of their souls. Their sins are not to be answered upon such as God hath sent to warn them to flee the wrath to come, and save themselves from this untoward generation. . . .

Thirdly, it should be the duty of an elder, when he enters into a house, to salute the master of that house, and if he gain his consent, then he may preach to all that are in that house; but if he gain not his consent, let him not go unto his slaves, or servants, but let the responsibility be upon the head of the master of that house, and the consequences thereof, and the guilt of that house is no longer upon his skirts, he is free; therefore, let him shake off the dust of his feet, and go his way. But if the master of that house give consent, the elder may preach to his family, his wife, his children and his servants, his man-servants, or his maid-servants, or his slaves; then it should be the duty of the elder to stand up boldly for the cause of Christ, and warn that people with one accord to repent and be baptized for the remission of sins, and for the Holy Ghost, always commanding them in the name of the Lord, in the spirit of meekness, to be kindly affectionate one toward another, that the fathers should be kind to their children, husbands to their wives, masters to their slaves or servants, children obedient to their parents, wives to their husband,

and slaves or servants to their masters. (*D.H.C.* II, 262-264)

Preach the Gospel and Avoid Disputes

Let the elders be exceedingly careful about unnecessarily disturbing and harrowing up the feelings of the people. Remember that your business is to preach the Gospel in all humility and meekness, and warn sinners to repent and come to Christ. Avoid contentions and vain disputes with men of corrupt minds who do not desire to know the truth. Remember that "it is a day of warning, and not a day of many words." If they receive not your testimony in one place, flee to another, remembering to cast no reflections, nor throw out any bitter sayings. If you do your duty, it will be just as well with you, as though all men embraced the Gospel.

Be careful about sending boys to preach the Gospel to the world; if they go let them be accompanied by someone who is able to guide them in the proper channel, lest they become puffed up, and fall under condemnation, and into the snare of the devil. Finally, in these critical times, be careful; call on the Lord day and night; beware of pride; beware of false brethren, who will creep in among you to spy out your liberties. Awake to righteousness, and sin not; let your light shine, and show yourselves workmen that need not be ashamed, rightly dividing the word of truth. Apply yourselves diligently to study, that your minds may be stored with all necessary information. (*D.H.C.* I, 468-469)

A Debate of Gospel Principles

When we arrived, some of the young elders were about engaging in a debate on the subject of miracles. The question—"Was it, or was it not, the design of Christ to establish his Gospel by miracles?" After an interesting debate of three hours or more, during which time much talent was displayed, it was decided, by the president of the debate, in the negative, which was a righteous decision.

I discovered in this debate, much warmth displayed, too much zeal for mastery, too much of that enthusiasm that characterizes a lawyer at the bar, who is determined to defend his cause, right or wrong. I therefore availed myself of this favorable opportunity to drop a few words upon this subject, by way of advice, that they might improve their minds and cultivate their powers of intellect in a proper manner, that they might not incur the displeasure of heaven; that they should handle sacred things very sacredly, and with due deference to the opinions of others, and with an eye single to the glory of God. (*D.H.C.* II, 317-318)

The Price for Preaching the Fulness of the Gospel

It always has been when a man was sent of God with the priesthood and he began to preach the fulness of the Gospel, that he was thrust out by his friends, who are ready to butcher him if he teach things which they imagine to be wrong; and Jesus was crucified upon this principle. (*D.H.C.* V, 425)

CHAPTER SEVEN

Zion, Jerusalem, and the Gathering

The Whole of America Is Zion

. . . You know there has been great discussion in relation to Zion—where it is, and where the gathering of the dispensation is, and which I am now going to tell you. The prophets have spoken and written upon it; but I will make a proclamation that will cover a broader ground. *The whole of America is Zion itself from north to south, and is described by the prophets, who declare that it is the Zion where the mountain of the Lord should be, and that it should be in the center of the land.* When elders shall take up and examine the old prophecies in the Bible, they will see it. (*D.H.C.* VI, 318-319)

The City of Zion and Jerusalem

. . . The city of Zion spoken of by David, in the one hundred and second Psalm, will be built upon the land of America, "And the ransomed of the Lord shall return, and come to Zion with songs and everlasting joy upon their heads." (Isaiah 35:10); and then they will be delivered from the overflowing scourge that shall pass through the land. But Judah shall obtain deliverance at Jerusalem. See Joel 2:32; Isaiah 26:20-21; Jeremiah 30:12; Psalm 1:5; Ezekiel 34:11-13. These are testimonies that the Good Shepherd will put forth his own sheep, and lead them out from all nations where they have been scattered in a cloudy and dark day, to Zion, and to Jerusalem; besides many more testimonies which might be brought. (*D.H.C.* I, 315)

The Land of Zion Designated

I received, by a heavenly vision, a commandment in June following, to take my journey to the western boundaries of the State of Missouri, and there designate the very spot which was to be the central place for the commencement of the gathering together of those who embrace the fulness of the everlasting Gospel. Accordingly I undertook the journey, with certain ones of my brethren, and after a long and tedious journey, suffering many privations and hardships, arrived in Jackson County, Missouri, and after viewing the country, seeking diligently at the hand of God, he manifested himself unto us, and designated, to me and others, the very spot upon which he designed to commence the work of the gathering, and the upbuilding of an "holy city," which should be called Zion—Zion, because it is a place of righteousness, and all who build thereon are to worship the true and living God, and all believe in one doctrine, even the doctrine of our Lord and Savior Jesus Christ. "Thy watchmen shall lift up the voice: with the voice together shall they sing: for they shall see eye to eye, when the Lord shall bring again Zion." (Isaiah 52:8)

. . . After having ascertained the very spot, and having the happiness of seeing quite a number of the families of my brethren comfortably situated upon the land, I took leave of them and journeyed back to Ohio, and used every influence and argument that lay in my power to get those who believed in the everlasting covenant, whose circumstances would admit, and whose families were willing to remove to the place which I had designated to be the land of Zion; and thus the sound of the gathering, and of the doctrine, went abroad into the world; . . . (D.H.C. II, 254-255)

Zion

I cannot learn from any communication by the Spirit to me, that Zion has forfeited her claim to a celestial crown, notwithstanding the Lord has caused her to be thus afflicted, except it may be some individuals, who have walked in disobedience, and forsaken the new covenant; all such will be made manifest by their works in due time. I have always expected that Zion would suffer some affliction, from what I could learn from the commandments which have been given. But I would remind you of a certain clause in one which says, that after *much* tribulation cometh the *blessing*. By this, and also others, and also one received of late, I know that Zion, in the due time of the Lord, will be redeemed; but how many will be the days of her purification, tribulation, and affliction, the Lord has kept hid from my eyes; and when I inquire concerning this subject, the voice of the Lord is: Be still, and know that I am God! all those who suffer for my name shall reign with me, and he that layeth down his life for my sake shall find it again.

Now, there are two things of which I am ignorant; and the Lord will not show them unto me, perhaps for a wise purpose in himself—I mean in some respects—and they are these: Why God has suffered so great a calamity to come upon Zion, and what the great moving cause of this great affliction is; and again, by what means he will return her back to her inheritance, with songs of everlasting joy upon her head. These two things, brethren, are in part kept back that they are not plainly shown unto me; but there are some things that are plainly manifest which have incurred the displeasure of the Almighty. (*D.H.C.* I, 453-454)

Why the Saints Are Gathered

This subject was presented to me since I came to the stand. What was the object of gathering the Jews, or the people of God in any age of the world? I can never find much to say in expounding a text. A man never has half so much fuss to unlock a door, if he has a key, as though he had not, and had to cut it open with his jackknife.

The main object was to build unto the Lord a house whereby he could reveal unto his people the ordinances of his house and the glories of his kingdom, and teach the people the way of salvation; for there are certain ordinances and principles that, when they are taught and practiced, must be done in a place or house built for that purpose.

It was the design of the councils of heaven before the world was, that the principles and laws of the priesthood should be predicated upon the gathering of the people in every age of the world. Jesus did everything to gather the people, and they would not be gathered, and he therefore poured out curses upon them. Ordinances instituted in the heavens before the foundation of the world, in the priesthood, for the salvation of men, are not to be altered or changed. All must be saved on the same principles.

It is for the same purpose that God gathers together his people in the last days, to build unto the Lord a house to prepare them for the ordinances and endowments, washings and anointings, etc. One of the ordinances of the house of the Lord is baptism for the dead. God decreed before the foundation of the world that that ordinance should be administered in a font prepared for that purpose in the house of the Lord. (*D.H.C.* V, 423-424)

"The Work of Gathering"

. . . All that the prophets that have written, from the days of righteous Abel, down to the last man that has left any testimony on record for our consideration, in speaking of the salvation of Israel in the last days, goes directly to show that it consists in the work of the gathering.

First, I shall begin by quoting from the prophecy of Enoch, speaking of the last days: "Righteousness will I send down out of heaven; and truth will I send forth out of the earth, to bear testimony of mine Only Begotten; his resurrection from the dead (this resurrection I understand to be the corporeal body); yea, and also the resurrection of all men; righteousness and truth will I cause to sweep the earth as with a flood, to gather out mine own elect from the four quarters of the earth, unto a place which I shall prepare, a Holy City, that my people may gird up their loins, and be looking forth for the time of my coming; for there shall be my tabernacle, and it shall be called Zion, a New Jerusalem." (Moses 7:62, 1902 edition)

Now I understand by this quotation, that God clearly manifested to Enoch the redemption which he prepared, by offering the Messiah as a Lamb slain from before the foundation of the world; and by virtue of the same, the glorious resurrection of the Savior, and the resurrection of all the human family, even a resurrection of their corporeal bodies, is brought to pass; and also righteousness and truth are to sweep the earth as with a flood. And now, I ask, how righteousness and truth are going to sweep the earth as with a flood? I will answer. Men and angels are to be co-workers in bringing to pass this great work, and Zion is to be prepared, even a new Jerusalem, for the elect that are to be gathered from the four quarters of the earth, and to be established an holy city, for the tabernacle of the Lord shall be with them.

Now Enoch was in good company in his views upon this subject: "And I heard a great voice out of heaven saying, Behold, the tabernacle of God is with men, and he will dwell with them, and they shall be his people, and God himself shall be with them, and be their God." (Rev. 21:3)

I discover by this quotation, that John upon the Isle of Patmos, saw the same things concerning the last days, which Enoch saw. But before the tabernacle can be with men, the elect must be gathered from the four quarters of the earth. And to show further upon this subject of the gathering, Moses, after having pronounced the blessing and cursing upon the children of Israel, for their obedience or disobedience, says thus:

"And it shall come to pass, when all these things are come upon thee, the blessing and the curse, which I have set before thee, and thou shalt call them to mind among all the nations whither the Lord thy God hath driven thee, And shalt return unto the Lord thy God, and shalt obey his voice according to all that I command thee, this day, thou and thy children, with all thine heart, and with all thy soul. That the Lord thy God will turn thy captivity, and have compassion upon thee, and will return and gather thee from all the nations, whither the Lord thy God hath scattered thee. If any of thine be driven out unto the outmost parts of heaven, from thence will the Lord thy God gather thee, and from thence will he fetch thee." (Deut. 30:1-4)

It has been said by many of the learned and wise men, or historians, that the Indians or aborigines of this continent are of the scattered tribes of Israel. It has been conjectured by many others, that the aborigines of this continent are not of the tribes of Israel, but the ten tribes have been led away into some unknown regions of the north. Let this be as it may, the prophecy I have just quoted "will fetch them," in the last days, and place them in the land which their fathers possessed. And you will find in Deuteronomy, "And the Lord thy God will put all these curses upon thine enemies, and on them that hate thee, which persecuted thee." (Ibid., 30:7.)

Many may say that this scripture is fulfilled, but let them mark carefully what the prophet says: "If any are driven out unto the outmost parts of heaven," (which must mean the breadth of the earth). Now this promise is good to any, if there should be such, that are driven out, even in the last days, therefore, the children of the fathers have claim unto this day. And if these curses are to be laid over on the heads of their enemies, wo be unto the Gentiles. (See Book of Mormon, III Nephi, 16.) "Wo unto the unbelieving of the Gentiles, saith the Father." And again (see Book of Mormon, Ibid., 20:22, which says),

"Behold this people will I establish in this land, unto the fulfilling of the covenant which I made with your father Jacob, and it shall be a New Jerusalem." Now we learn from the Book of Mormon the very identical continent and spot of land upon which the New Jerusalem is to stand, and it must be caught up according to the vision of John upon the Isle of Patmos.

Now many will feel disposed to say, that this New Jerusalem spoken of, is the Jerusalem that was built by the Jews on the eastern continent. But you will see, from Revelation 21:2, there was a New Jerusalem coming down from God out of heaven, adorned as a bride for her husband; that after this, the Revelator was caught away in the Spirit, to a great and high mountain, and saw the great and holy city descending out of heaven from God. Now there are two cities spoken of here. As everything cannot be had in so narrow a compass as a letter, I shall say with brevity, that there is a New Jerusalem to be established on this continent, and also Jerusalem shall be rebuilt on the eastern continent: "Behold, Ether saw the days of Christ, and he spake concerning the house of Israel, and the Jerusalem from whence Lehi should come; after it should be destroyed, it should be built up again, a holy city unto the Lord, wherefore it could not be a new Jerusalem, for it had been in a time of old." (See Ether 13:4-12.) This may suffice, upon the subject of gathering, until my next. (*D.H.C.* II, 260-262)

Gathering of the Saints to Precede Destructions upon the Earth

Take away the Book of Mormon and the revelations, and where is our religion? We have none; for without Zion, and a place of deliverance, we must fall; because the time is near when the sun will be darkened, and the moon turn to blood, and the stars fall from heaven, and the earth reel to and fro. Then, if this is the case, and if we are not sanctified and gathered to the places God has

appointed, with all our former professions and our great
love for the Bible, we must fall; we cannot stand; we cannot be saved; for God will gather out his Saints from the
Gentiles, and then comes desolation and destruction, and
none can escape except the pure in heart who are gathered.
(*D.H.C.* II, 52)

Gathering of the Saints

The greatest temporal and spiritual blessings which
always flow from faithfulness and concerted effort, never
attended individual exertion or enterprise. The history of
all past ages abundantly attests this fact. In addition to all
temporal blessings, there is no other way for the Saints
to be saved in these last days, [than by the gathering]
as the concurrent testimony of all the holy prophets clearly
proves, for it is written—"They shall come from the east,
and be gathered from the west; the north shall give up,
and the south shall keep not back." "The sons of God
shall be gathered from far, and his daughters from the
ends of the earth."

It is also the concurrent testimony of all the prophets,
that this gathering together of all the Saints, must take
place before the Lord comes to "take vengeance upon the
ungodly," and "to be glorified and admired by all those
who obey the Gospel." The fiftieth Psalm, from the first
to the fifth verse inclusive, describes the glory and majesty
of that event. (*D.H.C.* IV, 272)

The Gathering of Israel

Much has been said and done of late by the general
government in relation to the Indians (Lamanites) within
the territorial limits of the United States. One of the most
important points in the faith of the Church of the Latter-
day Saints, through the fulness of the everlasting Gospel,
is the gathering of Israel (of whom the Lamanites constitute a part) that happy time when Jacob shall go up

to the house of the Lord, to worship him in spirit and in truth, to live in holiness; when the Lord will restore his judges as at the first, and his counselors as at the beginning; when every man may sit under his own vine and fig tree, and there will be none to molest or make afraid; when he will turn to them a pure language, and the earth will be filled with sacred knowledge, as the waters cover the great deep; when it shall no longer be said, the Lord lives that brought up the children of Israel out of the land of Egypt, but the Lord lives that brought up the children of Israel from the land of the north, and from all the land whither he has driven them. That day is one, all important to all men.

In view of its importance, together with all that the prophets have said about it before us, we feel like dropping a few ideas in connection with the official statements from the government concerning the Indians. In speaking of the gathering, we mean to be understood as speaking of it according to scripture, the gathering of the elect of the Lord out of every nation on earth, and bringing them to the place of the Lord of Hosts, when the city of righteousness shall be built, and where the people shall be of one heart and one mind, when the Savior comes; yea, where the people shall walk with God like Enoch, and be free from sin. The word of the Lord is precious; and when we read that the veil spread over all nations will be destroyed, and the pure in heart see God, and reign with him a thousand years on earth, we want all honest men to have a chance to gather and build up a city of righteousness, where even [upon] the bells of the horses shall be written *Holiness to the Lord.*

The Book of Mormon has made known who Israel is, upon this continent. And while we behold the government of the United States gathering the Indians, and locating them upon lands to be their own, how sweet it is to think that they may one day be gathered by the Gospel! (*D.H.C.* II, 357-358)

CHAPTER EIGHT

Temple Work and Spiritual Blessings

Baptism for the Dead Introduced by the Prophet

I presume the doctrine of "baptism for the dead" has ere this reached your ears, and may have raised some inquiries in your minds respecting the same. I cannot in this letter give you all the information you may desire on the subject; but aside from knowledge independent of the Bible, I would say that it was certainly practiced by the ancient churches; and Paul endeavors to prove the doctrine of the resurrection from the same, and says, "Else what shall they do which are baptized for the dead, if the dead rise not at all? why are they then baptized for the dead?" (I Cor. 15:29)

I first mentioned the doctrine in public when preaching the funeral sermon of Brother Seymour Brunson; and have since then given general instructions in the Church on the subject. The Saints have the privilege of being baptized for those of their relatives who are dead, whom they believe would have embraced the Gospel, if they had been privileged with hearing it, and who have received the Gospel in the spirit, through the instrumentality of those who have been commissioned to preach to them while in prison.

Without enlarging on the subject, you will undoubtedly see its consistency and reasonableness; and it presents the Gospel of Christ in probably a more enlarged scale than some have imagined it. (*D.H.C.* IV, 231)

The Doctrine of Baptism for the Dead

The doctrine of baptism for the dead is clearly shown in the New Testament; and if the doctrine is not good, then throw the New Testament away; but if it is the word of God, then let the doctrine be acknowledged; and it was the reason why Jesus said unto the Jews, "How oft would I have gathered thy children together, even as a hen gathereth her chickens under her wings, and ye would not!" (See Matt. 23:37.)—that they might attend to the ordinances of baptism for the dead as well as other ordinances of the priesthood, and receive revelations from heaven, and be perfected in the things of the kingdom of God—but they would not. This was the case on the Day of Pentecost: those blessings were poured out on the disciples on that occasion. God ordained that he would save the dead and would do it by gathering his people together. (*D.H.C.* V, 425)

Man to Act as an Agent in Being Baptized for the Dead

. . . Again; if we can, by the authority of the priesthood of the Son of God, baptize a man in the name of the Father, of the Son, and of the Holy Ghost, for the remission of sins, it is just as much our privilege to act as an agent, and be baptized for the remission of sins for and in behalf of our dead kindred, who have not heard the Gospel, or the fulness of it. (*D.H.C.* IV, 569)

Baptism for the Dead

. . . Every man that has been baptized and belongs to the kingdom has a right to be baptized for those who have gone before; and as soon as the law of the Gospel is obeyed here by their friends who act as proxy for them, the Lord has administrators there to set them free. A man may act as proxy for his own relatives; the ordinances of the Gospel which were laid out before the foundations of the world have thus been fulfilled by them, and we may be baptized for those whom we have much friendship for; but it must first be revealed to the man of God, lest we should run too far. "As in Adam all die, even so in Christ shall all be made alive" (I Cor. 15:22); all shall be raised from the dead. The Lamb of God hath brought to pass the resurrection, so that all shall rise from the dead. (*D.H.C.* VI, 365-366)

The Doctrine of Baptism for the Dead Explained

President Joseph Smith, by request of the Twelve Apostles, gave instructions on the doctrine of baptism for the dead, which were listened to with intense interest by the large assembly. He presented baptism for the dead as the only way that men can appear as saviors on Mount Zion.

The proclamation of the first principles of the Gospel was a means of salvation to men individually; and it was the truth, not men, that saved them; but men, by actively engaging in rites of salvation substitutionally became instrumental in bringing multitudes of their kindred into the kingdom of God. (*D.H.C.* IV, 424-425)

We Are Commanded to Be Baptized for Our Dead

And now as the great purposes of God are hastening to their accomplishment, and the things spoken of in the prophets are fulfilling, as the kingdom of God is established on the earth, and the ancient order of things restored, the Lord has manifested to us this day and privilege, and we are commanded to be baptized for our dead, thus fulfilling the words of Obadiah, when speaking of the glory of the latter-day: "And saviours shall come up on mount Zion to judge the remnant of Esau, and the kingdom shall be the Lord's." (Obad.:21) A view of these things reconciles the scriptures of truth, justifies the ways of God to man, places the human family upon an equal footing, and harmonizes with every principle of righteousness, justice, and truth. We will conclude with the words of Peter: "For the time past of our life may suffice us to have wrought the will of the Gentiles." (I Pet. 4:3) "For, for this cause was the Gospel preached also to them that are dead, that they might be judged according to men in the flesh, but live according to God in the spirit." (*D.H.C.* IV, 599)

The Justice of Baptism for the Dead

The idea that some men form of the justice, judgment, and mercy of God, is too foolish for an intelligent man to think of: for instance, it is common for many of our orthodox preachers to suppose that if a man is not what they call converted, if he dies in that state he must remain eternally in hell without any hope. Infinite years in torment must be spent, and never, never, never have an end; and yet this eternal misery is made frequently to rest upon the merest casualty. The breaking of a shoestring, the tearing of a coat of those officiating, or the peculiar location in which a person lives, may be the means, indirectly of his damnation, or the cause of his not being saved. I will suppose a case which is not extraordinary: Two men, who have been equally wicked, who have neglected religion, are both of them taken sick at the same time; one of them has the good fortune to be visited by a praying man, and he gets converted a few minutes before he dies; the other sends for three different praying men, a tailor, a shoemaker, and a tinman; the tinman has a handle to solder to a can, the tailor has a buttonhole to work on some coat that he needed in a hurry, and the shoemaker has a patch to put on somebody's boot; then none of them can go in time, the man dies, and goes to hell: one of these is exalted to Abraham's bosom, he sits down in the presence of God and enjoys eternal, uninterrupted happiness, while the other, equally as good as he, sinks to eternal damnation, irretrievable misery and hopeless despair, because a man had a boot to mend, the buttonhole of a coat to work, or a handle to solder on to a saucepan.

The plans of Jehovah are not so unjust, the statements of holy writ so visionary, nor the plan of salvation for the human family so incompatible with common sense; at such proceedings God would frown with indignance, angels would hide their heads in shame, and every virtuous, intelligent man would recoil.

If human laws award to each man his deserts, and punish all delinquents according to their several crimes, surely the Lord will not be more cruel than man, for he is a wise legislator, and his laws are more equitable, his enactments more just, and his decisions more perfect than those of man; and as man judges his fellow man by law, and punishes him according to the penalty of the law, so does God of heaven judge "according to the deeds done in the body." To say that the heathens would be damned because they did not believe the Gospel would be preposterous, and to say that the Jews would all be damned that do not believe in Jesus would be equally absurd; for "how can they believe on him of whom they have not heard, and how can they hear without a preacher, and how can he preach except he be sent"; consequently neither Jew nor heathen can be culpable for rejecting the conflicting opinions of sectarianism, nor for rejecting any testimony but that which is sent of God, for as the preacher cannot preach except he be sent, so the hearer cannot believe without he hear a "sent" preacher, and cannot be condemned for what he has not heard, and being without law, will have to be judged without law.

When speaking about the blessings pertaining to the Gospel and the consequences connected with disobedience to the requirements, we are frequently asked the question, what has become of our fathers? Will they all be damned for not obeying the Gospel, when they never heard it? Certainly not. But they will possess the same privilege that we here enjoy, through the medium of the everlasting priesthood, which not only administers on earth, but also in heaven, and the wise dispensations of the great Jehovah;

hence those characters referred to by Isaiah will be visited by the priesthood, and come out of their prison upon the same principle as those who were disobedient in the days of Noah were visited by our Savior [who possessed the everlasting Melchizedek Priesthood] and had the Gospel preached to them, by him in prison; and in order that they might fulfil all the requisitions of God, living friends were baptized for their dead friends, and thus fulfilled the requirement of God, which says, "Except a man be born of water and of the Spirit, he cannot enter into the kingdom of God"; they were baptized, of course, not for themselves, but for their dead. (*D.H.C.* IV, 597-599)

Wisdom and Mercy of God Shown in the Doctrine of Temple Work for the Dead

. . . It is no more incredible that God should *save* the dead, than that he should *raise* the dead.

There is never a time when the spirit is too old to approach God. All are within the reach of pardoning mercy, who have not committed the unpardonable sin, which hath no forgiveness, neither in this world, nor in the world to come. There is a way to release the spirits of the dead; that is by the power and authority of the priesthood—by binding and loosing on earth. This doctrine appears glorious, inasmuch as it exhibits the greatness of divine compassion and benevolence in the extent of the plan of human salvation.

This glorious truth is well calculated to enlarge the understanding, and to sustain the soul under troubles, difficulties and distresses. For illustration, suppose the case of two men, brothers, equally intelligent learned, virtuous and lovely, walking in uprightness and in all good conscience, so far as they have been able to discern duty from the muddy stream of tradition, or from the blotted page of the book of nature.

One dies and is buried, having never heard the Gospel of reconciliation; to the other the message of salvation is sent; he hears and embraces it, and is made the heir of eternal life. Shall the one become the partaker of glory and the other be consigned to hopeless perdition? Is there no chance for his escape? Sectarianism answers "none." Such an idea is worse than atheism. The truth shall break down and dash in pieces all such bigoted Pharisaism; the sects shall be sifted, the honest in heart brought out, and their priests left in the midst of their corruption. . . .

This doctrine presents in a clear light the wisdom and mercy of God in preparing an ordinance for the salvation of the dead, being baptized by proxy, their names recorded in heaven and they judged according to the deeds done in the body. This doctrine was the burden of the scriptures. Those Saints who neglect it in behalf of their deceased relatives, do it at the peril of their own salvation. (*D.H.C.* IV, 425-426)

We Cannot Be Made Perfect without Our Dead

The kingdom of heaven is like a grain of mustard seed. The mustard seed is small, but brings forth a large tree, and the fowls lodge in the branches. The fowls are the angels. Thus angels come down, combine together to gather their children, and gather them. We cannot be made perfect without them, nor they without us; when these things are done, the Son of Man will descend, the Ancient of Days sit; we may come to an innumerable company of angels, have communion with and receive instructions from them. Paul told about Moses' proceedings; spoke of the children of Israel being baptized. (I Cor. 10:1-4) He knew this, and that all the ordinances and blessings were in the Church. Paul had these things, and we may have the fowls of heaven lodge in the branches, etc.

The "Horn" made war with the Saints and overcame them, until the Ancient of Days came; judgment was given to the Saints of the Most High from the Ancient of Days;

the time came that the Saints possessed the kingdom. This not only makes us ministers here, but in eternity. (*D.H.C.* III, 389)

Saviors on Mount Zion

The Bible says, "I will send you Elijah the prophet before the coming of the great and dreadful day of the Lord: And he shall turn the heart of the fathers to the children, and the heart of the children to the fathers, lest I come and smite the earth with a curse." (Mal. 4:5-6)

Now, the word *turn* here should be translated *bind,* or seal. But what is the object of this important mission? or how is it to be fulfilled? The keys are to be delivered, the spirit of Elijah is to come, the Gospel to be established, the Saints of God gathered, Zion built up, and the Saints to come up as saviors on Mount Zion.

But how are they to become saviors on Mount Zion? By building their temples, erecting their baptismal fonts, and going forth and receiving all the ordinances, baptisms, confirmations, washings, anointings, ordinations and sealing powers upon their heads, in behalf of all their progenitors who are dead, and redeem them that they may come forth in the first resurrection and be exalted to thrones of glory with them; and herein is the chain that binds the hearts of the fathers to the children, and the children to the fathers, which fulfils the mission of Elijah. And I would to God that this temple was now done, that we might go into it, and go to work and improve our time, and make use of the seals while they are on earth.

The Saints have not too much time to save and redeem their dead, and gather together their living relatives, that they may be saved also, before the earth will be smitten, and the consumption decreed falls upon the world.

I would advise all the Saints to go to with their might and gather together all their living relatives to this place, that they may be sealed and saved, that they may be prepared against the day that the destroying angel goes forth;

and if the whole Church should go to with all their might to save their dead, seal their posterity, and gather their living friends, and spend none of their time in behalf of the world, they would hardly get through before night would come, when no man can work; and my only trouble at the present time is concerning ourselves, that the Saints *will be divided, broken up, and scattered,* before we get our salvation secure; for there are so many fools in the world for the devil to operate upon, it gives him the advantage oftentimes.

The question is frequently asked, "Can we not be saved without going through with all those ordinances, etc.?" I would answer, No, not the fulness of salvation. Jesus said, "There are many mansions in my Father's house, and I will go and prepare a place for you." *House* here named should have been translated kingdom; and any person who is exalted to the highest mansion has to abide a celestial law, and the whole law, too.

But there has been a great difficulty in getting anything into the heads of this generation. It has been like splitting hemlock knots with a corn-dodger for a wedge, and a pumpkin for a beetle. Even the Saints are slow to understand.

I have tried for a number of years to get the minds of the Saints prepared to receive the things of God; but we frequently see some of them, after suffering all they have for the work of God, will fly to pieces like glass as soon as anything comes that is contrary to their traditions: they cannot stand the fire at all. How many will be able to abide a celestial law, and go through and receive their exaltation, I am unable to say, as many are called, but few are chosen. (*D.H.C.* VI, 183-185)

Man's Responsibility to His Progenitors

What promises are made in relation to the subject of the salvation of the dead? and what kind of characters are those who can be saved, although their bodies are moul-

dering and decaying in the grave? When his commandments teach us, it is in view of eternity; for we are looked
upon by God as though we were in eternity; God dwells
in eternity, and does not view things as we do.

The greatest responsibility in this world that God has
laid upon us is to seek after our dead. The apostle says,
"They without us cannot be made perfect"; for it is necessary that the sealing power should be in our hands to seal
our children and our dead for the fulness of the dispensation of times—a dispensation to meet the promises made
by Jesus Christ before the foundation of the world for
the salvation of man.

Now, I will speak of them. I will meet Paul halfway.
I say to you, Paul, you cannot be perfect without us. It
is necessary that those who are going before and those
who come after us should have salvation in common with
us; and thus hath God made it obligatory upon man.
Hence, God said, "I will send you Elijah the prophet before
the coming of the great and dreadful day of the Lord;
he shall turn the heart of the fathers to the children, and
the heart of the children to their fathers, lest I come and
smite the earth with a curse." (D.H.C. VI, 313)

Information Regarding the Endowment Given in 1835

The endowment you are so anxious about, you cannot
comprehend now, nor could Gabriel explain it to the
understanding of your dark minds; but strive to be prepared in your hearts, be faithful in all things, that when
we meet in the solemn assembly, that is, when such as
God shall name out of all the official members shall meet,
we must be clean every whit. Let us be faithful and silent,
brethren, and if God gives you a manifestation, keep it to
yourselves; be watchful and prayerful, and you shall have
a prelude of those joys that God will pour out on that day.
Do not watch for iniquity in each other, if you do you will
not get an endowment, for God will not bestow it on such.
But if we are faithful, and live by every word that pro-

ceeds forth from the mouth of God, I will venture to prophesy that we shall get a blessing that will be worth remembering, if we should live as long as John the Revelator; our blessings will be such as we have not realized before, nor received in this generation. The order of the house of God has been, and ever will be, the same, even after Christ comes; and after the termination of the thousand years it will be the same; and we shall finally enter into the celestial kingdom of God, and enjoy it forever.

You need an endowment, brethren, in order that you may be prepared and able to overcome all things; and those that reject your testimony will be damned. The sick will be healed, the lame made to walk, the deaf to hear, and the blind to see, through your instrumentality. But let me tell you, that you will not have power, after the endowment to heal those that have not faith, nor to benefit them, for you might as well expect to benefit a devil in hell as such as are possessed of his spirit, and are willing to keep it; for they are habitations for devils, and only fit for his society. But when you are endowed and prepared to preach the Gospel to all nations, kindred, and tongues, in their own languages, you must faithfully warn all, and bind up the testimony, and seal up the law, and the destroying angel will follow close at your heels, and exercise his tremendous mission upon the children of disobedience; and destroy the workers of iniquity, while the Saints will be gathered out from among them, and stand in holy places ready to meet the Bridegroom when he comes. (*D.H.C.* II, 309)

The Endowment to Be Received Only by the Spiritually Minded

I spent the day in the upper part of the store, that is in my private office (so called because in that room I keep my sacred writings, translate ancient records, and receive revelations) and in my general business office, or lodge room (that is where the Masonic fraternity meet occasionally, for want of a better place) in council with General James Adams, of Springfield, Patriarch Hyrum Smith, Bishops Newel K. Whitney and George Miller, and President Brigham Young and Elders Heber C. Kimball and Willard Richards, instructing them in the principles and order of the priesthood, attending to washings, anointings, endowments and the communication of keys pertaining to the Aaronic Priesthood, and so on to the highest order of the Melchizedek Priesthood setting forth the order pertaining to the Ancient of Days, and all those plans and principles by which anyone is enabled to secure the fulness of those blessings which have been prepared for the Church of the Firstborn, and come up and abide in the presence of the Eloheim in the eternal worlds. In this council was instituted the ancient order of things for the first time in these last days. And the communications I made to this council were of things spiritual, and to be received only by the spiritual minded: and there was nothing made known to these men but what will be made known to all the Saints of the last days, so soon as they are prepared to receive, and a proper place is prepared to communicate them, even to the weakest of the Saints; therefore let the Saints be diligent in building the temple, and all houses which they have been, or shall hereafter be, commanded of God to build; and wait their time with patience in all meekness, faith, perseverance unto the end, knowing assuredly that all these things referred to in this council are always governed by the principle of revelation. (*D.H.C.* V, 1-2)

Sealing Ordinances of the Gospel

In order for you to receive your children to yourselves you must have a promise—some ordinance; some blessing, in order to ascend above principalities, . . . (*D.H.C.* VI, 366)

Marriage for Eternity and Its Blessings

Except a man and his wife enter into an everlasting covenant and be married for eternity, while in this probation, by the power and authority of the Holy Priesthood, they will cease to increase when they die; that is, they will not have any children after the resurrection. But those who are married by the power and authority of the priesthood in this life, and continue without committing the sin against the Holy Ghost, will continue to increase and have children in the celestial glory. (*D.H.C.* V, 391)

Make Our Calling and Election Sure

Then I would exhort you to go on and continue to call upon God until you make your calling and election sure for yourselves, by obtaining this more sure word of prophecy, and wait patiently for the promise until you obtain it, etc. (*D.H.C.* V, 389)

Doctrines of Resurrection and Election

The doctrine of the resurrection of the dead and the eternal judgment are necessary to preach among the first principles of the Gospel of Jesus Christ.

The doctrine of election. Paul exhorts us to make our calling and election sure. This is the sealing power spoken of by Paul in other places.

"13. In whom ye also trusted, that after ye heard the word of truth, the gospel of your salvation: in whom also after that ye believed, ye were sealed with that holy Spirit of promise.

"14. Which is the earnest of our inheritance until the redemption of the purchased possession, unto the praise of his glory" (Eph. 1:13-14), that we may be sealed up unto the day of redemption.

This principle ought (in its proper place) to be taught, for God hath not revealed anything to Joseph, but what

he will make known unto the Twelve, and even the least
Saint may know all things as fast as he is able to bear
them, for the day must come when no man need say to
his neighbor, Know ye the Lord; for all shall know him
(*who remain*) from the least to the greatest. How is this
to be done? It is to be done by this sealing power, and
the other Comforter spoken of, which will be manifest
by revelation. (*D.H.C.* III, 379-380)

Doctrine of Election

He then spoke on the subject of election, and read
the 9th chapter of Romans, from which it was evident
that the election there spoken of was pertaining to the
flesh, and had reference to the seed of Abraham, according
to the promise God made to Abraham, saying, "In thee,
and in thy seed, all the families of the earth shall be
blessed." To them belonged the adoption and the covenants, etc. Paul said, when he saw their unbelief, "I wish
myself accursed"—according to the flesh—not according
to the spirit. Why did God say to Pharaoh, "For this cause
have I raised thee up"? Because Pharaoh was a fit instrument—a wicked man, and had committed acts of cruelty
of the most atrocious nature. The election of the promised
seed still continues, and in the last day, they shall have
the priesthood restored unto them, and they shall be the
"saviors on Mount Zion," the ministers of our God; if it
were not for the remnant which was left, then might men
now be as Sodom and Gomorrah. The whole of the chapter
had reference to the priesthood and the house of Israel;
and unconditional election of individuals to eternal life
was not taught by the apostles. God did elect or pre-
destinate, that all those who would be saved, should be
saved in Christ Jesus, and through obedience to the Gospel;
but he passes over no man's sins, but visits them with cor-
rection, and if his children will not repent of their sins
he will discard them. (*D.H.C.* IV, 359-360)

Doctrine of Election and Sealing

. . . When a seal is put upon the father and mother, it secures their posterity, so that they cannot be lost, but will be saved by virtue of the covenant of their father and mother. (*D.H.C.* V, 530)

Salvation for the Dead

. . . There must, however, be a place built expressly for that purpose, and for men to be baptized for their dead. It must be built in this the central place; for every man who wishes to save his father, mother, brothers, sisters and friends, must go through all the ordinances for each one of them separately, the same as for himself, from baptism to ordination, washings and anointings, and receive all the keys and powers of the priesthood, the same as for himself. (*D.H.C.* VI, 319)

Keys of the Kingdom

I preached in the grove on the keys of the kingdom, charity, etc. The keys are certain signs and words by which false spirits and personages may be detected from true, which cannot be revealed to the elders till the temple is completed. The rich can only get them in the temple, the poor may get them on the mountaintop as did Moses. The rich cannot be saved without charity, giving to feed the poor when and how God requires, as well as building. There are signs in heaven, earth and hell; the elders must know them all, to be endowed with power, to finish their work and prevent imposition. The devil knows many signs, but does not know the sign of the Son of Man, or Jesus. No one can truly say he knows God until he has handled something, and this can only be the holiest of holies. (*D.H.C.* IV, 608)

Visions and Blessings in the Kirtland Temple

I met the quorums in the evening and instructed them respecting the ordinance of washing of feet, which they were to attend to on Wednesday following; and gave them instructions in relation to the spirit of prophecy, and called upon the congregation to speak, and not to fear to prophesy good concerning the Saints, for if you prophesy the falling of these hills and the rising of the valleys, the downfall of the enemies of Zion and the rising of the kingdom of God, it shall come to pass. Do not quench the Spirit, for the first one that opens his mouth shall receive the spirit of prophecy.

Brother George A. Smith arose and began to prophesy, when a noise was heard like the sound of a rushing mighty wind, which filled the temple, and all the congregation simultaneously arose, being moved upon by an invisible power; many began to speak in tongues and prophesy; others saw glorious visions; and I beheld the temple was filled with angels, which fact I declared to the congregation. The people of the neighborhood came running together (hearing an unusual sound within, and seeing a bright light like a pillar of fire resting upon the temple), and were astonished at what was taking place. This continued until the meeting closed at eleven p.m.

The number of official members present on this occasion was four hundred and sixteen, being a greater number than ever assembled on any former occasion. (*D.H.C.* II, 428)

Redemption of Zion and Other Visions Witnessed in the Temple at Kirtland

. . . I also beheld the redemption of Zion, and many things which the tongue of man cannot describe in full.

Many of my brethren who received the ordinance with me saw glorious visions also. Angels ministered unto them as well as to myself, and the power of the Highest rested upon us; the house was filled with the glory of God, and we shouted hosanna to God and the Lamb. My scribe also received his anointing with us, and saw, in a vision, the armies of heaven protecting the Saints in their return to Zion, and many things which I saw.

The bishop of Kirtland with his counselors, and the bishop of Zion with his counselors, were present with us, and received their anointings under the hands of Father Smith, and this was confirmed by the Presidency, and the glories of heaven were unfolded to them also.

We then invited the high councilors of Kirtland and Zion into our room and President Hyrum Smith anointed the head of the president of the councilors in Kirtland, and President David Whitmer the head of the president of the councilors of Zion. The president of each quorum then anointed the heads of his colleagues, each in his turn, beginning at the oldest.

The visions of heaven were opened to them also. Some of them saw the face of the Savior, and others were ministered unto by holy angels, and the spirit of prophecy and revelation was poured out in mighty power; and loud hosannas, and glory to God in the highest, saluted the heavens, for we all communed with the heavenly host. And I saw in my vision all of the Presidency in the celestial kingdom of God, and many others that were present. . . . (*D.H.C. II*, 381-382)

CHAPTER NINE

Truth, Knowledge, and Salvation

Truth Is "Mormonism"

. . . Hell may pour forth its rage like the burning lava of mount Vesuvius, or of Etna, or of the most terrible of the burning mountains; and yet shall "Mormonism" stand. Water, fire, truth and God are all realities. Truth is "Mormonism." God is the author of it. He is our shield. It is by him we received our birth. It was by his voice that we were called to a dispensation of his Gospel in the beginning of the fulness of times. It was by him we received the Book of Mormon; and it is by him that we remain unto this day; and by him we shall remain, if it shall be for our glory; and in his Almighty name we are determined to endure tribulation as good soldiers unto the end. (*D.H.C.* III, 297)

The Power of Truth

. . . In relation to the power over the minds of mankind which I hold, I would say, [sic] It is in consequence of the power of truth in the doctrines which I have been an instrument in the hands of God of presenting unto them, and not because of any compulsion on my part. I wish to ask if ever I got any of it unfairly? if I have not reproved you in the gate? I ask, Did I ever exercise any compulsion over any man? Did I not give him the liberty of disbelieving any doctrine I have preached, if he saw fit? Why do not my enemies strike a blow at the doctrine? They cannot

do it: it is truth, and I defy all men to upset it. I am the
voice of one crying in the wilderness, "Repent ye of your
sins and prepare the way for the coming of the Son of Man;
for the kingdom of God has come unto you, and henceforth the ax is laid unto the root of the tree; and every
tree that bringeth not forth good fruit, God Almighty (and
not Joe Smith) shall hew it down and cast it into the fire."
(*D.H.C.* VI, 273-274)

Mormonism and Truth

Have the Presbyterians any truth? Yes. Have the
Baptists, Methodists, etc., any truth? Yes. They all have
a little truth mixed with error. We should gather all the
good and true principles in the world and treasure them
up, or we shall not come out true "Mormons." (*D.H.C.*
V, 517)

The Gospel Embraces All Truth

. . . I thank God for preserving me from my enemies;
I have no enemies but for the truth's sake. I have no
desire but to do all men good. I feel to pray for all men.
We don't ask any people to throw away any good they
have got; we only ask them to come and get more. What
if all the world should embrace this Gospel? They would
then see eye to eye, and the blessings of God would be
poured out upon the people, which is the desire of my
whole soul. (*D.H.C.* V, 259)

Liberty to Think and Believe Proposed by the Prophet

I will endeavor to instruct you in relation to the
meaning of the beasts and figures spoken of. I should
not have called up the subject had it not been for this
circumstance. Elder Pelatiah Brown, one of the wisest
old heads we have among us, and whom I now see before
me, has been preaching concerning the beast which was

full of eyes before and behind; and for this he was hauled up for trial before the high council.

I did not like the old man being called up for erring in doctrine. It looks too much like the Methodist, and not like the Latter-day Saints. Methodists have creeds which a man must believe or be asked out of their church. I want the liberty of thinking and believing as I please. It feels so good not to be trammelled. It does not prove that a man is not a good man because he errs in doctrine.

The high council undertook to censure and correct Elder Brown, because of his teachings in relation to the beasts. Whether they actually corrected him or not, I am a little doubtful, but don't care. Father Brown came to me to know what he should do about it. (*D.H.C.* V, 340)

In Knowledge There Is Power

In knowledge there is power. God has more power than all other beings, because he has greater knowledge; and hence he knows how to subject all other beings to him. He has power over all. (*D.H.C.* V, 340)

Knowledge Saves a Man

. . . Knowledge saves a man; and in the world of spirits no man can be exalted but by knowledge. So long as a man will not give heed to the commandments, he must abide without salvation. If a man has knowledge, he can be saved; although, if he has been guilty of great sins, he will be punished for them. But when he consents to obey the gospel, whether here or in the world of spirits, he is saved. (*D.H.C.* VI, 314)

Satan Cannot Be Blamed for Our Sins

He . . . observed that Satan was generally blamed for the evils which we did, but if he was the cause of all our wickedness, men could not be condemned. The devil could not compel mankind to do evil; all was voluntary. Those

who resisted the Spirit of God, would be liable to be led
into temptation, and then the association of heaven would
be withdrawn from those who refused to be made partakers of such great glory. God would not exert any com-
pulsory means, and the devil could not; and such ideas
as were entertained [on these subjects] by many were
absurd. (*D.H.C.* IV, 358)

The Contention in Heaven

The contention in heaven was—Jesus said there would
be certain souls that would not be saved; and the devil
said he would save them all, and laid his plans before the
grand council, who gave their vote in favor of Jesus Christ.
So the devil rose up in rebellion against God, and was
cast down, with all who put up their heads for him.
(*D.H.C.* VI, 314)

Obedience to God's Commandments Is Required
for Salvation

. . . to get salvation we must not only do some things,
but everything which God has commanded. Men may
preach and practice everything except those things which
God commands us to do, and will be damned at last. We
may tithe mint and rue, and all manner of herbs, and still
not obey the commandments of God. The object with me
is to obey and teach others to obey God in just what he
tells us to do. It mattereth not whether the principle is
popular or unpopular, I will always maintain a true
principle, even if I stand alone in it. (*D.H.C.* VI, 223)

Our Acts Are Recorded and Will Be Laid before Us at
a Future Day

Our acts are recorded, and at a future day they will
be laid before us, and if we should fail to judge right and
injure our fellow beings, they may there, perhaps, condemn
us; there they are of great consequence, and to me the
consequence appears to be of force, beyond anything which
I am able to express. (*D.H.C.* II, 26)

Some Too Wise to Be Taught

Many men will say, "I will never forsake you, but will stand by you at all times." But the moment you teach them some of the mysteries of the kingdom of God that are retained in the heavens and are to be revealed to the children of men when they are prepared for them, they will be the first to stone you and put you to death. It was this same principle that crucified the Lord Jesus Christ, and will cause the people to kill the prophets in this generation.

Many things are insoluble to the children of men in the last days: for instance, that God should raise the dead, and forgetting that things have been hid from before the foundation of the world, which are to be revealed to babes in the last days.

There are a great many wise men and women too in our midst who are too wise to be taught; therefore they must die in their ignorance, and in the resurrection they will find their mistake. Many seal up the door of heaven by saying, So far God may reveal and I will believe. (*D.H.C.* V, 424)

Salvation Based on a Knowledge of the Priesthood

Salvation is for a man to be saved from all his enemies; for until a man can triumph over death, he is not saved. A knowledge of the priesthood alone will do this. (*D.H.C.* V, 403)

Knowledge Cannot Be Imparted Unless the People Prepare Themselves to Receive

Paul ascended into the third heavens, and he could understand the three principal rounds of Jacob's ladder—the telestial, the terrestrial, and the celestial glories or kingdoms, where Paul saw and heard things which were not lawful for him to utter. I could explain a hundred-fold more than I ever have of the glories of the kingdoms manifested to me in the vision, were I permitted, and were the people prepared to receive them.

The Lord deals with this people as a tender parent with a child, communicating light and intelligence and the knowledge of his ways as they can bear it. (*D.H.C.* V, 402)

Knowledge of the Things of God Are Necessary for Salvation

. . . A man is saved no faster than he gets knowledge, for if he does not get knowledge, he will be brought into captivity by some evil power in the other world, as evil spirits will have more knowledge, and consequently more power than many men who are on the earth. Hence it needs revelation to assist us, and give us knowledge of the things of God. (*D.H.C.* IV, 588)

The Meaning of Salvation

Salvation means a man's being placed beyond the power of all his enemies. (*D.H.C.* V, 392)

Knowledge through Jesus Christ Is the Grand Key

Now, there is some grand secret here, and keys to unlock the subject. Notwithstanding the apostle exhorts them to add to their faith, virtue, knowledge, temperance, etc., yet he exhorts them to make their calling and election sure. And though they had heard an audible voice from heaven bearing testimony that Jesus was the Son of God, yet he says we have a more sure word of prophecy, whereunto ye do well that ye take heed as unto a light shining in a dark place. Now, wherein could they have a more sure word of prophecy than to hear the voice of God saying, This is my beloved Son, etc.

Now for the secret and grand key. Though they might hear the voice of God and know that Jesus was the Son of God, this would be no evidence that their election and calling was made sure, that they had part with Christ, and were joint heirs with him. They then would want that more sure word of prophecy, that they were sealed in the heavens and had the promise of eternal life in the kingdom of God. Then, having this promise sealed unto them, it was an anchor to the soul, sure, and steadfast. Though the thunders might roll and lightnings flash, and earthquakes bellow, and war gather thick around, yet this hope and knowledge would support the soul in every hour of trial, trouble and tribulation. Then knowledge through our Lord and Savior Jesus Christ is the grand key that unlocks the glories and mysteries of the kingdom of heaven. (*D.H.C.* V, 388-389)

Knowledge and Its Application

It is not wisdom that we should have all knowledge at once presented before us; but that we should have a little at a time; then we can comprehend it. President Smith then read the 2nd Epistle of Peter, 1st chapter, 16th to last verses, and dwelt upon the 19th verse with some remarks:

Add to your faith knowledge, etc. The principle of knowledge is the principle of salvation. This principle can be comprehended by the faithful and diligent; and everyone that does not obtain knowledge sufficient to be saved will be condemned. The principle of salvation is given us through the knowledge of Jesus Christ. (*D.H.C.* V, 387)

The Meaning of Salvation

Salvation is nothing more nor less than to triumph over all our enemies and put them under our feet. And when we have power to put all enemies under our feet in this world, and a knowledge to triumph over all evil spirits in the world to come, then we are saved, as in the case of Jesus, who was to reign until he had put all enemies under his feet, and the last enemy was death. . . . No person can have this salvation except through a tabernacle. (*D.H.C.* V. 387-388)

Saints Must Receive Chastisement

. . . Because we will not receive chastisement at the hand of the Prophet and Apostles, the Lord chastiseth us with sickness and death. Let not any man publish his own righteousness, for others can see that for him; sooner let him confess his sins, and then he will be forgiven, and he will bring forth more fruit. When a corrupt man is chastised he gets angry and will not endure it. The reason we do not have the secrets of the Lord revealed unto us, is because we do not keep them but reveal them; we do not keep our own secrets, but reveal our difficulties to the world, even to our enemies, then how would we keep the secrets of the Lord? I can keep a secret till doomsday. What greater love hath any man than that he lay down his life for his friend; then why not fight for our friend until we die? (*D.H.C.* IV, 478-479)

CHAPTER TEN

Angels, Spirits, and Eternal Life

Intelligence Exists Eternally

. . . Is it logical to say that the intelligence of spirits is immortal, and yet that it has a beginning? The intelligence of spirits had no beginning, neither will it have an end. That is good logic. That which has a beginning may have an end. There never was a time when there were not spirits; for they are co-equal [co-eternal] with our Father in heaven. . . .

Intelligence is eternal and exists upon a self-existent principle. It is a spirit from age to age and there is no creation about it. . . . (*D.H.C.* VI, 311)

Explanation of Eternal Existence

I want to reason more on the spirit of man; for I am dwelling on the body and spirit of man—on the subject of the dead. I take my ring from my finger and liken it unto the mind of man—the immortal part, because it had no beginning. Suppose you cut it in two; then it has a beginning and an end; but join it again, and it continues one eternal round. So with the spirit of man. As the Lord liveth, if it had a beginning, it will have an end. (*D.H.C.* VI, 311)

Spirits and Angels

Spirits can only be revealed in flaming fire or glory. Angels have advanced further, their light and glory being tabernacled; and hence they appear in bodily shape. The spirits of just men are made ministering servants to those who are sealed unto life eternal, and it is through them that the sealing power comes down.

Patriarch Adams is now one of the spirits of the just men made perfect; and, if revealed now, must be revealed in fire; and the glory could not be endured. Jesus showed himself to his disciples, and they thought it was his spirit, and they were afraid to approach his spirit. Angels have advanced higher in knowledge and power, than spirits. (*D.H.C.* VI, 51)

Spirits of the Just

. . . When men are prepared, they are better off to go hence. . . . The spirits of the just are exalted to a greater and more glorious work; hence they are blessed in their departure to the world of spirits. Enveloped in flaming fire, they are not far from us, and know and understand our thoughts, feelings, and motions, and are often pained therewith.

Flesh and blood cannot go there; but flesh and bones, quickened by the Spirit of God, can. (*D.H.C.* VI, 52)

The Abode of Spirits

The righteous and the wicked all go to the same world of spirits until the resurrection. "I do not think so," says one. If you will go to my house any time, I will take my lexicon and prove it to you.

The great misery of departed spirits in the world of spirits, where they go after death, is to know that they come short of the glory that others enjoy and that they might have enjoyed themselves, and they are their own accusers. "But," says one, "I believe in one universal heaven and hell, where all go, and are all alike, and equally miserable or equally happy."

What! where all are huddled together—the honorable, virtuous, and murderers, and whoremongers, when it is written that they shall be judged according to the deeds done in the body? But Paul informs us of three glories and three heavens. He knew a man that was caught up to the third heavens. Now, if the doctrine of the sectarian world, that there is but one heaven, is true, Paul, what do you tell that lie for, and say there are three? Jesus said unto his disciples, "In my Father's house are many mansions, if it were not so, I would have told you. I go to prepare a place for you. . . . And I will come and receive you unto myself; that where I am, there ye may be also." (John 14:2-3)

Any man may believe that Jesus Christ is the Son of God, and be happy in that belief, and yet not obey his commandments, and at last be cut down for disobedience to the Lord's righteous requirements. (*D.H.C.* V, 425-426)

Meaning of the Word "Paradise"

I will say something about the spirits in prison. There has been much said by modern divines about the words of Jesus (when on the cross) to the thief, saying, "This day shalt thou be with me in paradise." King James' translators make it out to say *paradise*. But what is paradise? It is a modern word: it does not answer at all to the original word that Jesus made use of. Find the original of the word *paradise*. You may as easily find a needle in a haymow. Here is a chance for battle, ye learned men. There is nothing in the original word in Greek from which this was taken that signified paradise; but it was—This day thou shalt be with me in the world of spirits; then I will teach you all about it and answer your inquiries. And Peter says he went and preached to the world of spirits (spirits in prison, I Peter, 3:14) so that they who would receive it could have it answered by proxy by those who live on the earth, etc. (*D.H.C.* V, 424-425)

Spiritual and Heavenly Worlds

The organization of the spiritual and heavenly worlds, and of spiritual and heavenly beings, was agreeable to the most perfect order and harmony: their limits and bounds were fixed irrevocably, and voluntarily subscribed to in their heavenly estate by themselves, and were by our first parents subscribed to upon the earth. Hence the importance of embracing and subscribing to principles of eternal truth by all men upon the earth that expect eternal life.

I assure the Saints that truth, in reference to these matters, can and may be known through the revelations of God in the way of his ordinances, and in answer to prayer. The Hebrew Church "came unto the spirits of just men made perfect, and unto an innumerable company of angels, unto God the Father of all, and to Jesus Christ, the Mediator of the new covenant." What did they learn by coming of the spirits of just men made perfect? Is it written? No. What they learned has not been and could not have been written. What object was gained by this communication with the spirits of the just? It was the established order of the kingdom of God: the keys of power and knowledge were with them to communicate to the Saints. Hence the importance of understanding the distinction between the spirits of the just and angels. (*D.H.C.* VI, 51)

Three Keys Regarding Eternal Progression

1st key: Knowledge is the power of salvation. 2nd key: Make your calling and election sure. 3rd key: It is one thing to be on the mount and hear the excellent voice, etc., etc., and another to hear the voice declare to you, You have a part and lot in that kingdom. (*D.H.C.* V, 403)

The Spirits of Men Are Eternal

. . . I would just remark, that the spirits of men are eternal, that they are governed by the same priesthood that Abraham, Melchizedek, and the Apostles were: that they are organized according to that priesthood which is everlasting, "without beginning of days or end of years"—that they all move in their respective spheres, and are governed by the law of God; that when they appear upon the earth they are in a probationary state, and are preparing, if righteous, for a future and greater glory; that the spirits of good men cannot interfere with the wicked beyond their prescribed bounds, for "Michael, the Archangel, dared not bring a railing accusation against the devil, but said, 'The Lord rebuke thee, Satan.'" (*D.H.C.* IV, 575-576)

The World of Spirits

I have a father, brothers, children, and friends who have gone to a world of spirits. They are only absent for a moment. They are in the spirit, and we shall soon meet again. The time will soon arrive when the trumpet shall sound. When we depart, we shall hail our mothers, fathers, friends, and all whom we love, who have fallen asleep in Jesus. There will be no fear of mobs, persecutions, or malicious lawsuits and arrests; but it will be an eternity of felicity. (*D.H.C.* VI, 316)

Angels and Ministering Spirits

He explained the difference between an angel and a ministering spirit; the one a resurrected or translated body, with its spirit ministering to embodied spirits—the other a disembodied spirit, visiting and ministering to disembodied spirits. Jesus Christ became a ministering spirit (while his body was lying in the sepulchre) to the spirits in prison, to fulfil an important part of his mission, without which he could not have perfected his work, or entered into his rest. After his resurrection he appeared as an angel to his disciples.

Translated bodies cannot enter into rest until they have undergone a change equivalent to death. Translated bodies are designed for future missions.

The angel that appeared to John on the Isle of Patmos was a translated or resurrected body [i.e. personage],

Jesus Christ went in body after his resurrection, to minister to resurrected bodies. There has been a chain of authority and power from Adam down to the present time. (*D.H.C.* IV, 425)

Importance of a Physical Body

"The first step in the salvation of man is the laws of eternal and self-existent principles. Spirits are eternal. At the first organization in heaven we were all present, and saw the Savior chosen and appointed and the plan of salvation made, and we sanctioned it.

"We came to this earth that we might have a body and present it pure before God in the celestial kingdom. The great principle of happiness consists in having a body. The devil has no body, and herein is his punishment. He is pleased when he can obtain the tabernacle of man, and when cast out by the Savior he asked to go into the herd of swine, showing that he would prefer a swine's body to having none.

"All beings who have bodies have power over those who have not. The devil has no power over us only as we permit him. The moment we revolt at anything which comes from God, the devil takes power. This earth will be rolled back into the presence of God, and crowned with celestial glory." (Franklin D. Richards, and Elder James A. Little, *A Compendium of the Doctrines of the Gospel,* 1925 Edition, p. 271)

Difference between the Body and the Spirit

. . . we shall find a very material difference between the body and the spirit; the body is supposed to be organized matter, and the spirit, by many, is thought to be immaterial, without substance. With this latter statement we should beg leave to differ, and state that spirit is a substance; that it is material, but that it is more pure, elastic and refined matter than the body; that it existed before the body, can exist in the body; and will exist separate from the body, when the body will be mouldering in the dust; and will in the resurrection, be again united with it. (*D.H.C.* IV, 575)

The Spirit of Man Eternal

The spirit of man is not a created being; it existed from eternity, and will exist to eternity. Anything created cannot be eternal; and earth, water, etc., had their existence in an elementary state, from eternity. Our Savior speaks of children and says, Their angels always stand before my Father. The Father called all spirits before him at the creation of man, and organized them. He (Adam) is the head, and was told to multiply. The keys were first given to him, and by him to others. He will have to give an account of his stewardship, and they to him. (*D.H.C.* III, 387)

Eternal Duration of Matter

You ask the learned doctors why they say the world was made out of nothing, and they will answer, "Doesn't the Bible say he *created* the world?" And they infer, from the word *create,* that it must have been made out of nothing. Now, the word *create* came from the word *baurau,* which does not mean to create out of nothing; it means to organize; the same as a man would organize materials and build a ship. Hence we infer that God had materials to organize the world out of chaos—chaotic matter, which is element, and in which dwells all the glory. Element had an existence from the time he had. The pure principles of element are principles which can never be destroyed; they may be organized and re-organized, but not destroyed. They had no beginning and can have no end. (*D.H.C.* VI, 308-309)

The Righteous Shall Be Exalted

He said he did not care how fast we run in the path of virtue; resist evil, and there is no danger; God, men, and angels will not condemn those that resist everything that is evil, and devils cannot; as well might the devil seek to dethrone Jehovah, as overthrow an innocent soul that resists everything which is evil. (*D.H.C.* IV, 605)

Eternal Duration of Matter

Speaking of eternal duration of matter, I said:

There is no such thing as immaterial matter. All spirit is matter, but is more fine or pure, and can only be discerned by purer eyes. We cannot see it, but when our bodies are purified, we shall see that it is all matter. (*D.H.C.* V, 393)

CHAPTER ELEVEN

The Signs of the Times and the Second Coming of the Savior

Time of the Second Coming of Christ Not Revealed to Man

I have asked of the Lord concerning his coming; and while asking the Lord, he gave a sign and said, "In the days of Noah I set a bow in the heavens as a sign and token that in any year that the bow should be seen the Lord would not come; but there should be seedtime and harvest during that year: but whenever you see the bow withdrawn, it shall be a token that there shall be famine, pestilence, and great distress among the nations, and that the coming of the Messiah is not far distant."

But I will take the responsibility upon myself to prophesy in the name of the Lord, that Christ will not come this year, as Father Miller has prophesied, for we have seen the bow; and I also prophesy, in the name of the Lord, that Christ will not come in forty years; and if God ever spoke by my mouth, he will not come in that length of time. Brethren, when you go home, write this down, that it may be remembered.

Jesus Christ never did reveal to any man the precise time that he would come. Go and read the scriptures, and you cannot find anything that specified the exact hour he would come; and all that say so are false teachers. (*D.H.C.* VI, 254)

Coming of the Son of Man

When I contemplate the rapidity with which the great and glorious day of the coming of the Son of Man advances, when he shall come to receive his Saints unto himself, where they shall dwell in his presence, and be crowned with glory and immortality; when I consider that soon the heavens are to be shaken, and the earth tremble and reel to and fro; and that the heavens are to be unfolded as a scroll when it is rolled up; and that every mountain and island are to flee away, I cry out in my heart. What manner of persons ought we to be in all holy conversation and godliness! (*D.H.C.* I, 442)

The Bow in the Cloud Is a Sign

. . . The Lord hath set the bow in the cloud for a sign that while it shall be seen, seedtime and harvest, summer and winter shall not fail; but when it shall disappear, woe to that generation, for behold the end cometh quickly. (*D.H.C.* V, 402)

The Sign of the Son of Man

I saw a notice in the Chicago *Express* that one Hyrum Redding had seen the sign of the Son of Man, etc.; and I wrote to the editor of the *Times and Seasons*, as follows:

The Sign of the Son of Man

SIR:—Among the many signs of the times and other strange things which are continually agitating the minds of men, I notice a small speculation in the Chicago *Express,* upon the certificate of one Hyrum Redding, of Ogle county, Illinois, stating that he has seen the sign of the Son of Man as foretold in the 24th chapter of Matthew.

The slanderous allusion of a "seraglio" like the Grand Turk, which the editor applies to me, he may take to himself, for, "out of the abundance of the heart the mouth speaketh." Every honest man who has visited the city of Nauvoo since it existed, can bear record of better things, and place me in the front ranks of those who are known to do good for the sake of goodness, and show all liars, hypocrites and abominable creatures that, while vice sinks them down to darkness and woe, virtue exalts me and the Saints to light and immortality.

The editor, as well as some others, "thinks that Joe Smith has his match at last," because Mr. Redding thinks that he has seen the sign of the Son of Man. But I shall use my right, and declare that, notwithstanding Mr. Redding may have seen a wonderful appearance in the clouds one morning about sunrise (which is nothing very uncommon in the winter season), he has not seen the sign of the Son of Man, as foretold by Jesus; neither has any man, nor will any man, until after the sun shall have been darkened and the moon bathed in blood; for the Lord hath not shown me any such sign; and as the prophet saith, so it must be—"Surely the Lord God will do nothing, but he revealeth his secret unto his servants the prophets." (See Amos 3:7.) Therefore hear this, O earth: The Lord will not come to reign over the righteous, in this world in 1843, nor until everything for the Bridegroom is ready.

Yours respectfully,
JOSEPH SMITH.

(*D.H.C.* V, 290-291)

No Peace but in Zion and Her Stakes in the Last Days

Men profess to prophesy. I will prophesy that the signs of the coming of the Son of Man are already commenced. One pestilence will desolate after another. We shall soon have war and bloodshed. The moon will be turned into blood. I testify of these things, and that the coming of the Son of Man is nigh, even at your doors. If our souls and our bodies are not looking forth for the coming of the Son of Man; and after we are dead, if we are not looking forth, we shall be among those who are calling for the rocks to fall upon them.

The hearts of the children of men will have to be turned to the fathers, and the fathers to the children, living or dead, to prepare them for the coming of the Son of Man. If Elijah did not come, the whole earth would be smitten.

There will be here and there a stake [of Zion] for the gathering of the Saints. Some may have cried peace, but the Saints and the world will have little peace from henceforth. Let this not hinder us from going to the stakes; for God has told us to flee, not dally, or we shall be scattered, one here, and another there. There your children shall be blessed, and you in the midst of friends where you may be blessed. The Gospel net gathers of every kind.

I prophesy, that that man who tarries after he has an opportunity of going, will be afflicted by the devil. Wars are at hand; we must not delay; but are not required to sacrifice. We ought to have the building up of Zion as our greatest object. When wars come, we shall have to flee to Zion. The cry is to make haste. The last revelation says, Ye shall not have time to have gone over the earth, until these things come. It will come as did the cholera, war, fires, and earthquakes; one pestilence after another, until the Ancient of Days comes, then judgment will be given to the Saints.

Whatever you may hear about me or Kirtland, take no notice of it; for if it be a place of refuge, the devil will use his greatest efforts to trap the Saints. You must make yourselves acquainted with those men who like Daniel pray three times a day toward the house of the Lord. Look to the Presidency and receive instruction. Every man who is afraid, covetous, will be taken in a snare. The time is soon coming, when no man will have any peace but in Zion and her stakes.

I saw men hunting the lives of their own sons, and brother murdering brother, women killing their own daughters, and daughters seeking the lives of their mothers. I saw armies arrayed against armies. I saw blood, desolation, fires. The Son of Man has said that the mother shall be against the daughter, and the daughter against the mother. These things are at our doors. They will follow the Saints of God from city to city. Satan will rage, and the spirit of the devil is now enraged. I know not how soon these things will take place; but with a view of them, shall I cry peace? No! I will lift up my voice and testify of them. How long you will have good crops, and the famine be kept off, I do not know; when the fig tree leaves, know then that the summer is nigh at hand. (*D.H.C.* III, 390-391)

The Prophet Comments upon This Dispensation

. . .—a day in which the God of heaven has begun to restore the ancient order of his kingdom unto his servants and his people—a day in which all things are concurring to bring about the completion of the fulness of the Gospel, a fulness of the dispensation of dispensations, even the fulness of times; a day in which God has begun to make manifest and set in order in his Church those things which have been, and those things which the ancient prophets and wise men desired to see but died without beholding them; a day in which those things begin to be made manifest, which have been hid from before the foundation of the world, and which Jehovah has promised should be made known in his own due time unto his servants, to prepare the earth for the return of his glory, even a celestial glory, and a kingdom of priests and kings to God and the Lamb, forever, on Mount Zion, and with him the hundred and forty and four thousand whom John the Revelator saw, all of which is to come to pass in the restitution of all things. (*D.H.C.* IV, 492-493)

Dispensation of Fulness of Times

. . . The Dispensation of the Fulness of Times will bring to light the things that have been revealed in all former dispensations; also other things that have not been before revealed. He shall send Elijah, the Prophet, etc., and restore all things in Christ. (*D.H.C.* IV, 426)

The Lord's Work in These Last Days

(FIRST PRESIDENCY ADDRESS)

The work of the Lord in these last days is one of vast magnitude and almost beyond the comprehension of mortals. Its glories are past description, and its grandeur unsurpassable. It is the theme which has animated the bosom of prophets and righteous men from the creation of the world down through every succeeding generation to the present time; and it is truly the Dispensation of the Fulness of Times, when all things which are in Christ Jesus, whether in heaven or on the earth, shall be gathered together in him, and when all things shall be restored, as spoken of by all the holy prophets since the world began; for in it will take place the glorious fulfilment of the promises made to the fathers, while the manifestations of the power of the Most High will be great, glorious, and sublime.

. . . The work which has to be accomplished in the last days is one of vast importance, and will call into action the energy, skill, talent, and ability of the Saints, so that it may roll forth with that glory and majesty described by the prophet; and will consequently require the concentration of the Saints, to accomplish work of such magnitude and grandeur.

The work of the gathering spoken of in the scriptures will be necessary to bring about the glories of the last dispensation. (*D.H.C.* IV, 185-186)

The Second Coming of Christ

. . . Were I going to prophesy, I would say the end [of the world] would not come in 1844, 5, or 6, or in forty years. There are those of the rising generation who shall not taste death till Christ comes.

I was once praying earnestly upon this subject, and a voice said unto me, "My son, if thou livest until thou art eighty-five years of age, thou shalt see the face of the Son of Man." I was left to draw my own conclusions concerning this; and I took the liberty to conclude that if I did live to that time, he would make his appearance. But I do not say whether he will make his appearance or I shall go where he is. I prophesy in the name of the Lord God, and let it be written—the Son of Man will not come in the clouds of heaven till I am eighty-five years old. Then read the 14th chapter of Revelation, 6th and 7th verses— "And I saw another angel fly in the midst of heaven, having the everlasting gospel to preach unto them that dwell on the earth, and to every nation, and kindred, and tongue, and people, saying with a loud voice, Fear God and give glory to him, for the hour of his judgment is come. And Hosea, 6th chapter, After two days, etc.,—2,520 years; which brings it to 1890. The coming of the Son of Man never will be—never can be till the judgments spoken of for this hour are poured out: which judgments are commenced. Paul says, "Ye are the children of the light, and not of the darkness, that that day should overtake you as a thief in the night." (See I Thess. 5:5, 2.) It is not the design of the Almighty to come upon the earth and crush it and grind it to powder, but he will reveal it to his servants and prophets.

Judah must return, Jerusalem must be rebuilt, and the temple, and water come out from under the temple, and the waters of the Dead Sea be healed. It will take some time to rebuild the walls of the city and the temple, etc.; and all this must be done before the Son of Man will make his appearance. There will be wars and rumors of wars, signs in the heavens above and on the earth beneath, the sun turned into darkness and the moon to blood, earthquakes in divers places, the seas heaving beyond their bounds; then will appear one grand sign of the Son of Man in heaven. But what will the world do? They will say it is a planet, a comet, etc. But the Son of Man will come as the sign of the coming of the Son of Man, which will be as the light of the morning cometh out of the east. (*D.H.C.* V, 336-337)

The End of the World Is the Destruction of the Wicked

. . . the end of the world is the destruction of the wicked, the harvest and the end of the world have an allusion directly to the human family in the last days, instead of the earth, as many have imagined; and that which shall precede the coming of the Son of Man, and the restitution of all things spoken of by the mouth of all the holy prophets since the world began; and the angels are to have something to do in this great work, for they are the reapers. As, therefore, the tares are gathered and burned in the fire, so shall it be in the end of the world; that is, as the servants of God go forth warning the nations, both priests and people, and as they harden their hearts and reject the light of truth, these first being delivered over to the buffetings of Satan, and the law and the testimony being closed up, as it was in the case of the Jews, they are left in darkness, and delivered over unto the day of burning; thus being bound up by their creeds, and their bands being made strong by their priests, are prepared for the fulfilment of the saying of the Savior—"The Son of man shall send forth his angels, and . . . gather out of his kingdom all things that offend, and them which do iniquity; And shall cast them into a furnace of fire: there shall be wailing and gnashing of teeth." (Matt. 13:42-43) We understand that the work of gathering together of the wheat into barns or garners, is to take place while the tares are being bound over, and preparing for the day of burning; that after the day of burnings, the righteous shall shine forth like the sun, in the kingdom of their Father. Who hath ears to hear, let him hear. (*D.H.C.* II, 271)

Nearness of the Fulfilment of the Signs of the Times

. . . The servants of God will not have gone over the nations of the Gentiles, with a warning voice, until the destroying angel will commence to waste the inhabitants of the earth, and as the prophet hath said, "It shall be a vexation to hear the report." I speak thus because I feel for my fellow men; I do it in the name of the Lord, being moved upon by the Holy Spirit. Oh, that I could snatch them from the vortex of misery, into which I behold them plunging themselves, by their sins; that I might be enabled by the warning voice, to be an instrument of bringing them to unfeigned repentance, that they might have faith to stand in the evil day! (*D.H.C.* II, 263)

The Righteous Shall Suffer Persecution

. . . the destinies of all people are in the hands of a just God, and he will do no injustice to anyone; and this one thing is sure, that they who will live godly in Christ Jesus, shall suffer persecution; and before their robes are made white in the blood of the Lamb, it is to be expected, according to John the Revelator, they will pass through great tribulation. (*D.H.C.* I, 449)

Saints Will Not Escape All Judgments

After others had spoken I spoke and explained concerning the uselessness of preaching to the world about great judgments, but rather to preach the simple Gospel. Explained concerning the coming of the Son of Man; also that it is a false idea that the Saints will escape all the judgments, whilst the wicked suffer; for all flesh is subject to suffer, and "the righteous shall hardly escape"; still many of the Saints will escape, for the just shall live by faith; yet many of the righteous shall fall a prey to disease, to pestilence, etc., by reason of the weakness of the flesh, and yet be saved in the kingdom of God. So that it is an unhallowed principle to say that such and such have transgressed because they have been preyed upon by the disease or death, for all flesh is subject to death; and the Savior has said, "Judge not, lest ye be judged." (*D.H.C.* IV, 11)

The Days of Tribulation Are Fast Approaching

We have all been children, and are too much so at the present time; but we hope in the Lord that we may grow in grace and be prepared for all things which the bosom of futurity may disclose unto us. Time is rapidly rolling on, and the prophecies must be fulfilled. The days of tribulation are fast approaching, and the time to test the fidelity of the Saints has come. Rumor with her ten thousand tongues is diffusing her uncertain sounds in almost every ear; but in these times of sore trial, let the Saints be patient and see the salvation of God. Those who cannot endure persecution, and stand in the day of affliction, cannot stand in the day when the Son of God shall burst the veil, and appear in all the glory of his Father, with all the holy angels. (*D.H.C.* I, 468)

Men Must Become Harmless before the Brute Creation

In pitching my tent we found three massasaugas or prairie rattlesnakes, which the brethren were about to kill, but I said, "Let them alone—don't hurt them! How will the serpent ever lose its venom, while the servants of God possess the same disposition, and continue to make war upon it? Men must become harmless before the brute creation, and when men lose their vicious dispositions and cease to destroy the animal race, the lion and the lamb can dwell together, and the sucking child can play with the serpent in safety." The brethren took the serpents carefully on sticks and carried them across the creek. I exhorted the brethren not to kill a serpent, bird, or an animal of any kind during our journey unless it became necessary in order to preserve ourselves from hunger. (*D.H.C.* II, 71-72)

The Battle of Gog and Magog

The battle of Gog and Magog will be after the millennium. The remnant of all the nations that fight against Jerusalem were commanded to go up to Jerusalem to worship in the millennium. (*D.H.C.* V, 298)

Chapter Twelve

Death and Resurrection

Death a Blessing

. . . The only difference between the old and young dying is, one lives longer in heaven and eternal light and glory than the other, and is freed a little sooner from this miserable wicked world. (*D.H.C.* IV, 554)

Death of Infants

. . . The Lord takes many away, even in infancy, that they may escape the envy of man, and the sorrows and evils of this present world; they were too pure, too lovely, to live on earth; therefore, if rightly considered, instead of mourning we have reason to rejoice as they are delivered from evil, and we shall soon have them again. (*D.H.C.* IV, 553)

The Fundamental Parts of One's Body Never Become a Part of Another's Body

. . . There is no fundamental principle belonging to a human system that ever goes into another in this world or in the world to come; I care not what the theories of men are. We have the testimony that God will raise us up, and he has the power to do it. If anyone supposes that any part of our bodies, that is, the fundamental parts thereof, ever goes into another body, he is mistaken. (*D.H.C.* V, 339)

Resurrection of the Dead

. . . They must rise just as they died; we can there hail our lovely infants with the same glory—the same loveliness in the celestial glory, where they all enjoy alike. They differ in stature, in size, the same glorious spirit gives them the likeness of glory and bloom; the old man with his silvery hairs will glory in bloom and beauty. No man can describe it to you—no man can write it. (*D.H.C.* VI, 366)

Resurrection and Exaltation Explained

My text is on the resurrection of the dead, which you will find in the 14th chapter of John—"In my Father's house are many mansions." It should be—"In my Father's kingdom are many kingdoms," in order that ye may be heirs of God and joint-heirs with me. I do not believe the Methodist doctrine of sending honest men and noble-minded men to hell, along with the murderer and the adulterer. They may hurl all their hell and fiery billows upon me, for they will roll off me as fast as they come on. But I have an order of things to save the poor fellows at any rate, and get them saved; for I will send men to preach to them in prison and save them if I can.

There are mansions for those who obey a celestial law, and there are other mansions for those who come short of the law every man in his own order. There is baptism, etc., for those to exercise who are alive, and baptism for the dead who die without the knowledge of the Gospel.

I am going on in my progress for eternal life. It is not only necessary that you should be baptized for your dead, but you will have to go through all the ordinances for them, the same as you have gone through to save yourselves. There will be 144,000 saviors on Mount Zion, and with them an innumerable host that no man can number. Oh! I beseech you to go forward, go forward and make your calling and your election sure; and if any man preach any other Gospel than that which I have preached, he shall be cursed; and some of you who now hear me shall see it, and know that I testify the truth concerning them. (*D.H.C.* VI, 365)

The Place Where a Man Is Buried Is Sacred

I would esteem it one of the greatest blessings, if I am to be afflicted in this world to have my lot cast where I can find brothers and friends all around me. But this is not the thing I referred to: it is to have the privilege of having our dead buried on the land where God has appointed to gather his Saints together, and where there will be none but Saints, where they may have the privilege of laying their bodies where the Son of Man will make his appearance, and where they may hear the sound of the trump that shall call them forth to behold him, that in the morn of the resurrection they may come forth in a body, and come up out of their graves and strike hands immediately in eternal glory and felicity, rather than be scattered thousands of miles apart. There is something good and sacred to me in this thing. The place where a man is buried is sacred to me. This subject is made mention of in the Book of Mormon and other scriptures. Even to the aborigines of this land, the burying places of their fathers are more sacred than anything else.

When I heard of the death of our beloved Brother Barnes, it would not have affected me so much, if I had the opportunity of burying him in the land of Zion.

I believe those who have buried their friends here, their condition is enviable. Look at Jacob and Joseph in Egypt, how they required their friends to bury them in the tomb of their fathers. See the expense which attended the embalming and the going up of the great company to the burial.

It has always been considered a great calamity not to obtain an honorable burial: and one of the greatest curses the ancient prophets could put on any man, was that he should go without a burial. (*D.H.C.* V, 361)

The Prophet Desired to Be Buried with His People

I have said, Father, I desire to die here among the Saints. But if this is not thy will, and I go hence and die, wilt thou find some kind friend to bring my body back, and gather my friends who have fallen in foreign lands, and bring them up hither, that we may all lie together.

I will tell you what I want. If tomorrow I shall be called to lie in yonder tomb, in the morning of the resurrection let me strike hands with my father, and cry, "My father," and he will say, "My son, my son," as soon as the rock rends and before we come out of our graves.

And may we contemplate these things so? Yes, if we learn how to live and how to die. When we lie down we contemplate how we may rise in the morning; and it is pleasing for friends to lie down together, locked in the arms of love, to sleep and wake in each other's embrace and renew their conversation. (*D.H.C.* V, 361)

A Vision of the Resurrection

Would you think it strange if I relate what I have seen in vision in relation to this interesting theme? Those who have died in Jesus Christ may expect to enter into all that fruition of joy when they come forth, which they possessed or anticipated here.

So plain was the vision, that I actually saw men, before they had ascended from the tomb, as though they were getting up slowly. They took each other by the hand and said to each other, "My father, my son, my mother, my daughter, my brother, my sister." And when the voice calls for the dead to arise, suppose I am laid by the side of my father, what would be the first joy of my heart? To meet my father, my mother, my brother, my sister; and when they are by my side, I embrace them and they me.

It is my meditation all the day, and more than my meat and drink, to know how I shall make the Saints of God comprehend the visions that roll like an overflowing surge before my mind. (*D.H.C.* V, 361-362)

All Losses Will Be Made up in the Resurrection

. . . All your losses will be made up to you in the resurrection, provided you continue faithful. By the vision of the Almighty I have seen it. (*D.H.C.* V, 362)

Death Not to Be Feared

More painful to me are the thoughts of annihilation than death. If I have no expectation of seeing my father, mother, brothers, sisters and friends again, my heart would burst in a moment, and I should go down to my grave.

The expectation of seeing my friends in the morning of the resurrection cheers my soul and makes me bear up against the evils of life. It is like their taking a long journey, and on their return we meet them with increased joy. (*D.H.C.* V, 362)

Doctrine of the Resurrection Revealed from Heaven

God has revealed his Son from the heavens and the doctrine of the resurrection also; and we have a knowledge that those we bury here God will bring up again, clothed upon and quickened by the Spirit of the great God; and what mattereth it whether we lay them down, or we lay down with them, when we can keep them no longer? Let these truths sink down in our hearts, that we may even here begin to enjoy that which shall be in full hereafter.

Hosanna, hosanna, hosanna to Almighty God, that rays of light begin to burst forth upon us even now. I cannot find words in which to express myself. I am not learned, but I have as good feelings as any man.

O that I had the language of the archangel to express my feelings once to my friends! But I never expect to in this life. When others rejoice, I rejoice; when they mourn, I mourn. (*D.H.C.* V, 362)

Death and the Resurrection

All men know that they must die. And it is important that we should understand the reasons and causes of our exposure to the vicissitudes of life and of death, and the designs and purposes of God in our coming into the world, our sufferings here, and our departure hence. What is the object of our coming into existence, then dying and falling away, to be here no more? It is but reasonable to suppose that God would reveal something in reference to the matter, and it is a subject we ought to study more than any other. We ought to study it day and night, for the world is ignorant in reference to their true condition and relation. If we have any claim on our Heavenly Father for anything, it is for knowledge on this important subject. Could we read and comprehend all that has been written from the days of Adam, on the relation of man to God and angels in a future state, we should know very little about it. Reading the experience of others, or the revelation given to *them,* can never give *us* a comprehensive view of our condition and true relation to God. Knowledge of these things can only be obtained by experience through the ordinances of God set forth for that purpose. Could you gaze into heaven five minutes, you would know more than you would by reading all that ever was written on the subject.

We are only capable of comprehending that certain things exist, which we may acquire by certain fixed principles. If men would acquire salvation, they have got to be subject, before they leave this world, to certain rules and principles, which were fixed by an unalterable decree before the world was.

The disappointment of hopes and expectations at the resurrection would be indescribably dreadful. (*D.H.C.* VI, 50-51)

Assurance Given Regarding the Resurrection

I could go back and trace every object of interest concerning the relationship of man to God, if I had time. I can enter into the mysteries; I can enter largely into the eternal worlds; for Jesus said, "In my Father's house are many mansions; if it were not so, I would have told you. I go to prepare a place for you." (John 14:2) Paul says, "There is one glory of the sun, and another glory of the moon, and another glory of the stars; for one star differeth from another star in glory. So also is the resurrection of the dead." (I Cor. 15:41) What have we to console us in relation to the dead? We have reason to have the greatest hope and consolation for our dead of any people on the earth; for we have seen them walk worthily in our midst, and seen them sink asleep in the arms of Jesus; and those who have died in the faith are now in the celestial kingdom of God. And hence is the glory of the sun.

You mourners have occasion to rejoice, speaking of the death of Elder King Follett; for your husband and father is gone to wait until the resurrection of the dead— until the perfection of the remainder; for at the resurrection your friend will rise in perfect felicity and go to celestial glory, while many must wait myriads of years before they can receive the like blessings; and your expectations and hopes are far above what man can conceive; for why has God revealed it to us?

I am authorized to say, by the authority of the Holy Ghost, that you have no occasion to fear, for he is gone to the home of the just. Don't mourn, don't weep. I know it by the testimony of the Holy Ghost that is within me; and you may wait for your friends to come forth to meet you in the morn of the celestial world. (*D.H.C.* VI, 315)

Will Mothers Have Their Children in Eternity?

. . . "Will mothers have their children in eternity?" Yes! Yes! Mothers, you shall have your children; for they shall have eternal life, for their debt is paid. There is no damnation awaiting them for they are in the spirit. But as the child dies, so shall it rise from the dead, and be forever living in the learning of God. It will never grow [in

the grave]; it will still be the child, in the same precise
form [when it rises] as it appeared before it died out of
its mother's arms, but possessing all the intelligence of a
God. Children dwell in the mansions of glory and exercise power, but appear in the same form as when on earth.
Eternity is full of thrones, upon which dwell thousands
of children, reigning on thrones of glory, with not one
cubit added to their stature.*

(*It is clearly evident that in this passage concerning
little children and their salvation and glorification after
the resurrection, we do not have from the brethren, who
made the notes, a perfect report on the status of little
children after the resurrection. There was some lack of
interpretation in the report of the Prophet's remarks, for
he taught that little children would come forth from the
dead in the same form and size in which their bodies were
laid down but that they would grow after the resurrection
to the full stature of the spirit. For an account of this
teaching those who desire to investigate the matter more
fully may consult the *Documentary History of the Church*,
Vol. 4:556-7 and the footnote, (*D.H.C.* VI, 316)

The Resurrection

As concerning the resurrection, I will merely say that
all men will come from the grave as they lie down, whether
old or young; there will not be "added unto their stature
one cubit," neither taken from it; all will be raised by the
power of God, having spirit in their bodies, and not blood.
Children will be enthroned in the presence of God and
the Lamb with bodies of the same stature that they had
on earth, having been redeemed by the blood of the Lamb;
they will there enjoy the fulness of that light, glory and
intelligence, which is prepared in the celestial kingdom.
"Blessed are the dead who die in the Lord, for they rest
from their labors and their works do follow them." (*D.H.C.*
IV, 555-556)

Resurrection of Children

. . . President Woodruff very emphatically said on the occasion of the subject being agitated about 1888-9, that the Prophet taught subsequently to his King Follett sermon that children while resurrected in the stature at which they died would develop to the full stature of men and women after the resurrection; and that the contrary impression created by the report of the Prophet's King Follett sermon was due to a misunderstanding of his remarks and erroneous reporting. In addition to this personal recollection of the writer as to the testimony of the late President Wilford Woodruff, the following testimony of Elder Joseph Horne and his wife, M. Isabella Horne, on the same subject is important. The statements here copied were delivered in the presence of President Angus M. Cannon, of the Salt Lake Stake of Zion, and Elder Arthur Winter, at the residence of Brother Horne, in Salt Lake City, on November 19, 1896, and were reported stenographically by Arthur Winter, the Church official reporter.

Sister M. Isabella Horne said:

"In conversation with the Prophet Joseph Smith once in Nauvoo, the subject of children in the resurrection was broached. I believe it was in Sister Leonora Cannon Taylor's house. She had just lost one of her children, and I had also lost one previously. The Prophet wanted to comfort us, and he told us that we should receive those children in the morning of the resurrection just as we laid them down, in purity and innocence, and we should nourish and care for them as their mothers. He said that children would be raised in the resurrection just as they were laid down, and that they would obtain all the intelligence necessary to occupy thrones, principalities and powers. The idea that I got from what he said was that the children would grow and develop in the millennium, and that the mothers would have the pleasure of training and caring for them, which they had been deprived of in this life.

"This was sometime after the King Follett funeral, at which I was present."

Brother Joseph Horne said:

"I heard the Prophet Joseph Smith say that mothers should receive their children just as they laid them down, and that they would have the privilege of doing for them what they could not do here, the Prophet remarked: 'How would you know them if you did not receive them as you laid them down?' I also got the idea that children would grow and develop after the resurrection and that the mothers would care for them and train them."

We hereby certify that the foregoing is a full, true and correct account of the statements made by Joseph and M. Isabella Horne on the subject mentioned.

ANGUS M. CANNON.
ARTHUR WINTER.

We have read the foregoing, and certify that it is correct.

JOSEPH HORNE.
M. ISABELLA HORNE.

(*D.H.C.* IV, 556-557)

Christ and the Resurrected Saints during the Millennium

. . . I said, Christ and the resurrected Saints will reign over the earth during the thousand years. They will not probably dwell upon the earth, but will visit it when they please, or when it is necessary to govern it. There will be wicked men on the earth during the thousand years. The heathen nations who will not come up to worship will be visited with the judgments of God, and must eventually be destroyed from the earth. (*D.H.C.* V, 212)

Resurrection and Degrees of Glory

Go and read the vision in the Book of Covenants. There is clearly illustrated glory upon glory—one glory of the sun, another glory of the moon, and a glory of the stars; and as one star differeth from another star in glory, even so do they of the telestial world differ in glory, and every man who reigns in celestial glory is a God to his dominions. . . .

Paul says, "There is one glory of the sun, and another glory of the moon, and another glory of the stars; for one star differeth from another star in glory. So is also the resurrection of the dead." They who obtain a glorious resurrection from the dead, are exalted far above principalities, powers, thrones, dominions and angels, and are expressly declared to be heirs of God and joint heirs with Jesus Christ, all having eternal power. (*D.H.C.* VI, 477-478)

Joseph Smith's Views regarding the Vision of Glories

Nothing could be more pleasing to the Saints upon the order of the kingdom of the Lord, than the light which burst upon the world through the foregoing vision. Every law, every commandment, every promise, every truth, and every point touching the destiny of man, from Genesis to Revelation, where the purity of the scriptures remain unsullied by the folly of men, go to show the perfection of the theory (of different degrees of glory in the future life) and witness the fact that the document is a transcript from the records of the eternal world. The sublimity of the ideas; the purity of the language; the scope for action; the continued duration for completion, in order that the heirs of salvation may confess the Lord and bow the knee; the rewards for faithfulness, and the punishments for sins, are so much beyond the narrow-mindedness of men, that every man is constrained to exclaim: "It came from God." (*D.H.C.* I, 252-253)

CHAPTER THIRTEEN

Wickedness, Apostasy, and Evil Spirits

Man Is His Own Tormentor and Condemner

A man is his own tormentor and his own condemner. Hence the saying, They shall go into the lake that burns with fire and brimstone. The torment of disappointment in the mind of man is as exquisite as a lake burning with fire and brimstone. I say, so is the torment of man. (*D.H.C.* VI, 314)

Those Who Reject the Gospel Will Be Damned

[Observe] . . . Christendom at the present day, and where are they, with all their boasted religion, piety, and sacredness while at the same time they are crying out against prophets, apostles, angels, revelations, prophesying and visions, etc. Why, they are just ripening for the damnation of hell. They will be damned, for they reject the most glorious principle of the Gospel of Jesus Christ and treat with disdain and trample under foot the key that unlocks the heavens and puts in our possession the glories of the celestial world. Yes, I say, such will be damned, with all their professed godliness. (*D.H.C.* V, 389)

Evils of Immorality

. . . I was present with several of the Twelve, and gave an address tending to do away with every evil, and exhorting them to practice virtue and holiness before the

Lord; told them that the Church had not received any permission from me to commit fornication, adultery, or any corrupt action; but my every word and action has been to the contrary. If a man commit adultery, he cannot receive the celestial kingdom of God. Even if he is saved in any kingdom, it cannot be the celestial kingdom. (*D.H.C.* VI, 81)

The Devil Rebuked by the Prophet

"I also told him of our vision of the evil spirits in England on the opening of the Gospel to that people. He then gave me a relation of many contests that he had had with Satan, and his power that had been manifested from time to time since the commencement of bringing forth the Book of Mormon. I will relate one circumstance that took place at Far West, in a house that Joseph had purchased, which had been formerly occupied as a public house by some wicked people. A short time after he got into it, one of his children was taken very sick; he laid his hands upon the child, when it got better; as soon as he went out of doors, the child was taken sick again; he again laid his hands upon it, so that it again recovered. This occurred several times, when Joseph inquired of the Lord what it all meant; then he had an open vision, and saw the devil in person, who contended with Joseph face to face, for some time. He said it was his house, it belonged to him, and Joseph had no right there. Then Joseph rebuked Satan in the name of the Lord, and he departed and touched the child no more." (Orson F. Whitney, *Life of Heber C. Kimball*, 269-270)

The Second Death

Hear it, all ye ends of the earth—all ye priests, all ye sinners, and all men. Repent! Repent! Obey the Gospel. Turn to God; for your religion won't save you, and you will be damned. I do not say how long. There have been remarks made concerning all men being redeemed from hell; but I say that those who sin against the Holy Ghost cannot be forgiven in this world or in the world to come; they shall die the second death. Those who commit the unpardonable sin are doomed to *Gnolom*—to dwell in hell, worlds without end. As they concocted scenes of bloodshed in this world, so they shall rise to that resurrection which is as the lake of fire and brimstone. Some shall rise to the everlasting burnings of God; for God dwells in everlasting burnings and some shall rise to the damnation of their own filthiness, which is as exquisite a torment as the lake of fire and brimstone. (*D.H.C.* VI, 317)

What a Man Must Do to Commit the Unpardonable Sin

All sins shall be forgiven, except the sin against the Holy Ghost; for Jesus will save all except the sons of perdition. What must a man do to commit the unpardonable sin? He must receive the Holy Ghost, have the heavens opened unto him, and know God, and then sin against him. After a man has sinned against the Holy Ghost, there is no repentance for him. He has got to say that the sun does not shine while he sees it; he has got to deny Jesus Christ when the heavens have been opened unto him, and to deny the plan of salvation with his eyes open to the truth of it; and from that time he begins to be an enemy. This is the case with many apostates of the Church of Jesus Christ of Latter-day Saints.

When a man begins to be an enemy to this work, he hunts me, he seeks to kill me, and never ceases to thirst for my blood. He gets the spirit of the devil—the same spirit that they had who crucified the Lord of life—the same spirit that sins against the Holy Ghost. You cannot save such persons; you cannot bring them to repentance; they make open war, like the devil, and awful is the consequence. (*D.H.C.* VI, 314-315)

The Unpardonable Sin

. . . The unpardonable sin is to shed innocent blood, or be accessory thereto. All other sins will be visited with judgment in the flesh, and the spirit being delivered to the buffetings of Satan until the day of the Lord Jesus. (*D.H.C.* V, 391-392)

Salvation for All except Those Who Have Committed the Unpardonable Sin

I have a declaration to make as to the provisions which God hath made to suit the conditions of man—made from before the foundation of the world. What has Jesus said? All sins, and all blasphemies and every transgression, except one, that man can be guilty of, may be forgiven; and there is a salvation for all men, either in this world or the world to come, who have not committed the unpardonable sin, there being a provision either in this world or the world of spirits. Hence God hath made a provision that every spirit in the eternal world can be ferreted out and saved unless he has committed that unpardonable sin which cannot be remitted to him either in this world or the world of spirits. God has wrought out a salvation for all men, unless they have committed a certain sin; and every man who has a friend in the eternal world can save him, unless he has committed the unpardonable sin. And so you can see how far you can be a savior.

A man cannot commit the unpardonable sin after the dissolution of the body, and there is a way possible for escape.

. . . no man can commit the unpardonable sin after the dissolution of the body, nor in this life, until he receives the Holy Ghost; but they must do it in this world. Hence the salvation of Jesus Christ was wrought out for all men, in order to triumph over the devil; for if it did not catch him in one place, it would in another; for he stood up as a Savior. All will suffer until they obey Christ himself. (*D.H.C.* VI, 313-314)

Corruption in the Prophet's Day

I prophesy, in the name of the Lord God of Israel, anguish and wrath and tribulation and the withdrawing of the Spirit of God from the earth await this generation, until they are visited with utter desolation. This generation is as corrupt as the generation of the Jews that crucified Christ; and if he were here today, and should preach the same doctrine he did then, they would put him to death. I defy all the world to destroy the work of God; and I prophesy they never will have power to kill me till my work is accomplished, and I am ready to die. (*D.H.C.* VI, 58)

Meaning of the Word "Hell"

I will now turn linguist. There are many things in the Bible which do not, as they now stand, accord with the revelations of the Holy Ghost to me.

I will criticise a little further. There has been much said about the word *hell,* and the sectarian world have preached much about it, describing it to be a burning lake of fire and brimstone. But what is hell? It is another modern term, and is taken from *hades.* I'll hunt after hades as Pat did for the woodchuck.

Hades, the Greek, or *Shaole,* the Hebrew: these two significations mean a world of spirits. Hades, Shaole, paradise, spirits in prison, are all one: it is a world of spirits. (*D.H.C.* V, 425)

Punishment of the Devil

The spirits in the eternal world are like the spirits in this world. When those have come into this world and received tabernacles, then died and again have risen and received glorified bodies, they will have an ascendency

over the spirits who have received no bodies, or kept not
their first estate, like the devil. The punishment of the
devil was that he should not have a habitation like men.
The devil's retaliation is, he comes into this world, binds
up men's bodies, and occupies them himself. When the
authorities come along, they eject him from a stolen
habitation. (*D.H.C.* V, 403)

The Devil and His Work

Now, in this world, mankind are naturally selfish,
ambitious and striving to excel one above another; yet
some are willing to build up others as well as themselves.
So in the other world there are a variety of spirits. Some
seek to excel. And this was the case with Lucifer when
he fell. He sought for things which were unlawful. Hence
he was sent down, and it is said he drew many away with
him; and the greatness of his punishment is that he shall
not have a tabernacle. This is his punishment. So the
devil, thinking to thwart the decree of God, by going up
and down in the earth, seeking whom he may destroy—
any person that he can find that will yield to him, he will
bind him, and take possession of the body and reign there,
glorying in it mightily, not caring that he had got merely
a stolen body; and by-and-by someone having authority
will come along and cast him out and restore the tabernacle to its rightful owner. The devil steals a tabernacle
because he has not one of his own: but if he steals one,
he is always liable to be turned out of doors. (*D.H.C.*
V, 388)

Do Not Sin against the Holy Ghost Nor Prove a Traitor to the Brethren

O ye Twelve! and all Saints! profit by this important
Key—that in all your trials, troubles, temptations, afflictions, bonds, imprisonments and death, see to it, that you
do not betray heaven; that you do not betray Jesus Christ;
that you do not betray the brethren; that you do not betray

the revelations of God, whether in the Bible, Book of Mormon, or Doctrine and Covenants, or any other that ever was or ever will be given and revealed unto man in this world or that which is to come. Yea, in all your kicking and flounderings, see to it that you do not this thing, lest innocent blood be found upon your skirts, and you go down to hell. All other sins are not to be compared to sinning against the Holy Ghost, and proving a traitor to the brethren. (*D.H.C.* III, 385)

The Sign of Apostasy

I will give you one of the *keys* of the mysteries of the kingdom. It is an eternal principle, that has existed with God from all eternity: That man who rises up to condemn others, finding fault with the Church, saying that they are out of the way, while he himself is righteous, then know assuredly, that that man is in the high road to apostasy; and if he does not repent, will apostatize, as God lives. The principle is as correct as the one that Jesus put forth in saying that he who seeketh a sign is an adulterous person; and that principle is eternal, undeviating, and firm as the pillars of heaven; for whenever you see a man seeking after a sign, you may set it down that he is an adulterous man. (*D.H.C.* III, 385)

Traitors and Apostates

I testify again, as the Lord lives, God never will acknowledge any traitors or apostates. Any man who will betray the Catholics will betray you; and if he will betray me, he will betray you. (*D.H.C.* VI, 478)

Relationship of Catholic and Protestant

The old Catholic church traditions are worth more than all you have said. Here is a principle of logic that most men have no more sense than to adopt. I will illustrate it by an old apple tree. Here jumps off a branch and says, I am the true tree, and you are corrupt. If the whole tree is corrupt, are not its branches corrupt? If the Catholic religion is a false religion, how can any true religion come out of it? If the Catholic church is bad, how can any good thing come out of it? The character of the old churches have always been slandered by all apostates since the world began. (*D.H.C.* VI, 478)

Suspense—The Punishment of the Wicked

There is no pain so awful as that of suspense; this is the punishment of the wicked; their doubt, anxiety and suspense cause weeping, wailing and gnashing of teeth. (*D.H.C.* V, 340)

A Sign Seeker Is an Adulterous Man

When I was preaching in Philadelphia, a Quaker called out for a sign. I told him to be still. After the sermon, he again asked for a sign. I told the congregation the man was an adulterer; that a wicked and adulterous generation seeketh after a sign; and that the Lord had said to me in a revelation, that any man who wanted a sign was an adulterous person. "It is true," cried one, "for I caught him in the very act," which the man afterwards confessed, when he was baptized. (*D.H.C.* V, 268)

Wicked Men Will Assail the Servants of God in the Last Days

. . . He that will war the true Christian warfare against the corruptions of these last days will have wicked men and angels of devils, and all the infernal powers of darkness continually arrayed against him. When wicked and corrupt men oppose, it is a criterion to judge, if a man is warring the Christian warfare. When all men speak evil of you falsely, blessed are ye, etc. Shall a man be considered bad when men speak evil of him? No. If a man stands and opposes the world of sin, he may expect to have all wicked and corrupt spirits arrayed against him. But it will be but a little season, and all these afflictions will be turned away from us, inasmuch as we are faithful, and are not overcome by these evils. By seeing the blessings of the endowment rolling on, and the kingdom increasing and spreading from sea to sea, we shall rejoice that we were not overcome by these foolish things. (*D.H.C.* V, 141)

Wicked Spirits

It would seem also, that wicked spirits have their bounds, limits, and laws by which they are governed or controlled, and know their future destiny; hence, those that were in the maniac said to our Savior, "Art thou come to torment us before the time," and when Satan presented himself before the Lord, among the sons of God, he said that he came "from going to and fro in the earth, and from wandering up and down in it"; and he is emphatically called the prince of the power of the air; and, it is very evident that they possess a power that none but those who have the priesthood can control, as we have before adverted to, in the case of the sons of Sceva. (*D.H.C.* IV, 576)

The Devil, His Angels, and Sons of Perdition

Say to the brothers Hulet and to all others, that the Lord never authorized them to say that the devil, his angels, or the sons of perdition, should ever be restored; for their state of destiny was not revealed to man, is not revealed, nor ever shall be revealed, save to those who are made partakers thereof; consequently those who teach this doctrine have not received it of the Spirit of the Lord. Truly Brother Oliver declared it to be the doctrine of devils. We, therefore, command that this doctrine be taught no more in Zion. We sanction the decision of the bishop and his council, in relation to this doctrine being a bar to communion. (*D.H.C.* I, 366)

The Curse Upon Cain

. . . I referred to the curse of Ham for laughing at Noah while in his wine, but doing no harm. Noah was a righteous man, and yet he drank wine and became intoxicated; the Lord did not forsake him in consequence thereof, for he retained all the power of his priesthood, and when he was accused by Canaan, he cursed him by the priesthood which he held, and the Lord had respect to his word, and the priesthood which he held, notwithstanding he was drunk, and the curse remains upon the posterity of Canaan until the present day. (*D.H.C.* IV, 445-446)

Murderers Cannot Be Forgiven until They Have Paid the "Last Farthing"

. . . Peter preached repentance and baptism for the remission of sins to the Jews who had been led to acts of violence and blood by their leaders; but to the rulers he said, "I would that through ignorance ye did it, as did also those ye ruled." "Repent, therefore, and be converted, that your sins may be blotted out, when the times of refreshing (redemption) shall come from the presence of the Lord, for he shall send Jesus Christ, who before was preached unto you." The time of redemption here had reference to the time when Christ should come; then, and not till then, would their sins be blotted out. Why? Because they were murderers, and no murderer hath eternal life. Even David must wait for those times of refreshing, before he can come forth and his sins be blotted out. For Peter, speaking of him says, "David hath not yet ascended into heaven, for his sepulchre is with us to this day." His remains were then in the tomb. Now, we read that many bodies of the Saints arose at Christ's resurrection, probably all the Saints, but it seems that David did not. Why? Because he had been a murderer. If the ministers of religion had a proper understanding of the doctrine of eternal judgment, they would not be found attending the man who forfeited his life to the injured laws of his country, by shedding innocent blood; for such characters cannot be forgiven until they have paid the last farthing. The prayers of all the ministers in the world can never close the gates of hell against a murderer. (*D.H.C.* IV, 359)

Appearance of a Wicked Spirit to a Sister of the Church

There have also been ministering angels in the Church which were of Satan appearing as an angel of light. A sister in the state of New York had a vision, who said it was told her that if she would go to a certain place in the woods, an angel would appear to her. She went at the appointed time, and saw a glorious personage descending, arrayed in white, with sandy-colored hair; he commenced and told her to fear God, and said that her husband was called to do great things, but that he must not go more than one hundred miles from home or he would not return; whereas God had called him to go to the ends of the earth, and he has since been more than one thousand miles from home, and is yet alive. Many true things were spoken by this personage, and many things that were false. How, it may be asked, was this known to be a bad angel? By the color of his hair; that is one of the signs that he can be known by, and by his contradicting a former revelation. (*D.H.C.* IV, 581)

Try the Spirits and Prove Them

We may look for angels and receive their ministrations, but we are to try the spirits and prove them, for it is often the case that men make a mistake in regard to these things. God has so ordained that when he has communicated, no vision is to be taken but what you see by the seeing of the eye, or what you hear by the hearing of the ear. When you see a vision, pray for the interpretation; if you get not this, shut it up; there must be certainty in this matter. An open vision will manifest that which is more important. Lying spirits are going forth in the earth. There will be great manifestations of spirits, both false and true.

Being born again comes by the Spirit of God through ordinances. An angel of God never has wings. Some will say that they have seen a spirit; that he offered them his hand, but they did not touch it. This is a lie. First, it is contrary to the plan of God: a spirit cannot come but in glory; an angel has flesh and bones; we see not their glory. The devil may appear as an angel of light. Ask God to reveal it; if it be of the devil, he will flee from you: if of God, he will manifest himself, or make it manifest. We may come to Jesus and ask him; he will know all about it; if he comes to a little child, he will adapt himself to the language and capacity of a little child.

Every spirit, or vision, or singing, is not of God. The devil is an orator; he is powerful; he took our Savior on to a pinnacle of the temple, and kept him in the wilderness for forty days. The gift of discerning spirits will be given to the Presiding Elder. Pray for him that he may have this gift. Speak not in the gift of tongues without understanding it, or without interpretation. The devil can speak in tongues; the adversary will come with his work; he can tempt all classes; can speak in English or Dutch. Let no one speak in tongues unless he interpret, except by the consent of the one who is placed to preside; then he may discern or interpret, or another may. Let us seek for the glory of Abraham, Noah, Adam, the apostles, who have communion with [knowledge of] these things, and then we shall be among that number when Christ comes. (*D.H.C.* III, 391-392)

Enemies of the Gospel

It is thought by some that our enemies would be satisfied with my destruction; but I tell you that as soon as they have shed my blood they will thirst for the blood of every man in whose heart dwells a single spark of the spirit of the fulness of the Gospel. The opposition of these men is moved by the spirit of the adversary of all righteousness. It is not only to destroy me, but every man and woman who dares believe the doctrines that God hath inspired me to teach to this generation. (*D.H.C.* VI, 498)

CHAPTER FOURTEEN

Love

Love

Love is one of the chief characteristics of Deity, and ought to be manifested by those who aspire to be the sons of God. A man filled with the love of God is not content with blessing his family alone, but ranges through the whole world, anxious to bless the whole human race. (*D.H.C.* IV, 227)

Friendship and Love Unite the Human Family

Friendship is one of the grand fundamental principles of "Mormonism"; [it is designed] to revolutionize and civilize the world, and cause wars and contentions to cease and men to become friends and brothers. Even the wolf and the lamb shall dwell together; the leopard shall lie down with the kid, the calf, the young lion and the fatling; and a little child shall lead them; the bear and the cow shall lie down together, and the sucking child shall play on the hole of the asp, and the weaned child shall play on the cockatrice's den; and they shall not hurt or destroy in all my holy mountains, saith the Lord of hosts. (Isaiah.)

It is a time-honored adage that love begets love. Let us pour forth love—show forth our kindness unto all mankind, and the Lord will reward us with everlasting increase; cast our bread upon the waters and we shall receive it after many days, increased to a hundredfold. Friendship is like Brother Turley in his blacksmith shop welding iron to iron; it unites the human family with its happy influence. (*D.H.C.* V, 517)

The Principle of Love

Joseph remarked that all was well between him and the heavens; that he had no enmity against anyone; and as the prayer of Jesus, or his pattern, so prayed Joseph—"Father, forgive me my trespasses as I forgive those who trespass against me," for I freely forgive all men. If we would secure and cultivate the love of others, we must love others, even our enemies as well as friends.

Sectarian priests cry out concerning me, and ask, "Why is it this babbler gains so many followers, and retains them?" I answer, It is because I possess the principle of love. All I can offer the world is a good heart and a good hand.

The Saints can testify whether I am willing to lay down my life for my brethren. If it has been demonstrated that I have been willing to die for a "Mormon." I am bold to declare before heaven that I am just as ready to die in defending the rights of a Presbyterian, a Baptist, or a good man of any other denomination; for the same principle which would trample upon the rights of the Latter-day Saints would trample upon the rights of the Roman Catholics, or of any other denomination who may be unpopular and too weak to defend themselves.

It is a love of liberty which inspires my soul—civil and religious liberty to the whole of the human race. Love of liberty was diffused into my soul by my grandfathers while they dandled me on their knees; and shall I want friends? No. (*D.H.C.* V, 498)

Saints Must Love One Another

. . . It is a duty which every Saint ought to render to his brethren freely—to love them always, and ever succor them. To be justified before God we must love one another: we must overcome evil; we must visit the fatherless and the widow in their affliction, and we must keep ourselves unspotted from the world: for such virtues flow from the great fountain of pure religion. Strengthening our faith by adding every good quality that adorns the children of the blessed Jesus, we can pray in the season of prayer; we can love our neighbor as ourselves, and be faithful in tribulation, knowing that the reward of such is greater in the kingdom of heaven. What a consolation! What a joy! Let me live the life of the righteous, and let my reward be like his! (*D.H.C.* II, 229)

Love of Husbands and Wives

"Wives, submit yourselves unto your own husbands, as unto the Lord. For the husband is the head of the wife, even as Christ is the head of the church: and he is the saviour of the body. Therefore as the church is subject unto Christ, so let the wives be to their own husbands in every thing. Husbands, love your wives, even as Christ also loved the Church and gave himself for it; That he might sanctify and cleanse it with the washing of water by the word, That he might present it to himself a glorious church, not having spot, or wrinkle, or any such thing; but that it should be holy and without blemish. So ought men to love their own wives as their own bodies. He that loveth his wife, loveth himself. For no man ever yet hated his own flesh; but nourisheth and cherisheth it, even as the Lord the church: for we are members of his body, of his flesh, and of his bones. For this cause shall a man leave his father and mother, and shall be joined unto his wife, and they two shall be one flesh." (Eph. 5:22-31)

"Wives, submit yourselves unto your own husbands, as it is fit in the Lord. Husbands, love your wives, and be not bitter against them. Children, obey your parents, in all things, for this is well pleasing unto the Lord. Fathers, provoke not your children to anger, lest they be discouraged. Servants, obey in all things your masters, according to the flesh; not with eyeservice, as manpleasers, but in singleness of heart, fearing God." (Colossians 3:18-22) (*D.H.C.* II, 264)

Sisters to Have Confidence in and Love for Their Husbands

He exhorted the sisters always to concentrate their faith and prayers for, and place confidence in their husbands, whom God has appointed for them to honor, and in those faithful men whom God has placed at the head of the Church to lead his people; that we should arm and sustain them with our prayers; for the keys of the kingdom are about to be given to them, that they may be able to detect everything false; as well as to all the elders who shall prove their integrity in due season. . . .

How precious are the souls of men! The female part of the community are apt to be contracted in their views. You must not be contracted, but you must be liberal in your feelings. Let this [Relief] Society teach women how to behave towards their husbands, to treat them with mildness and affection. When a man is borne down with trouble, when he is perplexed with care and difficulty, if he can meet a smile instead of an argument or a murmur —if he can meet with mildness, it will calm down his soul and soothe his feelings; when the mind is going to despair, it needs a solace of affection and kindness. . . .

When you go home, never give a cross or unkind word to your husbands, but let kindness, charity and love crown your works henceforward; don't envy the finery and fleeting show of sinners, for they are in a miserable situation; but as far as you can, have mercy on them, for in a short time God will destroy them, if they will not repent and turn unto him. (*D.H.C.* IV, 604-605, 606-607)

Meekness, Love and Purity Advocated

. . . If you live up to your privileges, the angels cannot be restrained from being your associates. Females, [these remarks were made to the Relief Society] if they are pure and innocent, can come in the presence of God; for what is more pleasing to God than innocence; you must be innocent, or you cannot come up before God: if we would come before God, we must keep ourselves pure, as he is pure.

The devil has great power to deceive; he will so transform things as to make one gape at those who are doing the will of God. You need not be teasing your husbands because of their deeds, but let the weight of your innocence, kindness and affection be felt, which is more mighty than a millstone hung about the neck; not war, not jangle, not contradiction, or dispute, but meekness, love, purity—these are the things that should magnify you in the eyes of all good men. (*D.H.C.* IV, 605)

CHAPTER FIFTEEN

Prophets and Prophecy

Definition of a Prophet

If any person should ask me if I were a prophet, I should not deny it, as that would give me the lie; for, according to John, the testimony of Jesus is the spirit of prophecy; therefore, if I profess to be a witness or teacher, and have not the spirit of prophecy, which is the testimony of Jesus, I must be a false witness; but if I be a true teacher and witness, I must possess the spirit of prophecy, and that constitutes a prophet; and any man who says he is a teacher or preacher of righteousness, and denies the spirit of prophecy, is a liar, and the truth is not in him; and by this key false teachers and impostors may be detected. (*D.H.C.* V, 215-216)

A Prophet Not Always a Prophet

. . . I read German, and visited with a brother and sister from Michigan, who thought that "a prophet is always a prophet"; but I told them that a prophet was a prophet only when he was acting as such. (*D.H.C.* V, 265)

A Prophecy by Joseph Smith

I . . . gave a relation of my situation at the time I obtained the record (Book of Mormon), the persecutions I met with, and prophesied that I would stand and shine like the sun in the firmament, when my enemies and the gainsayers of my testimony shall be put down and cut off, and their names blotted out from among men. (*D.H.C.* II, 26)

Joseph Smith's Grandfather Predicted a Prophet Would Come Forth from His Family

My grandfather, Asael Smith, long ago predicted that there would be a prophet raised up in his family, and my grandmother was fully satisfied that it was fulfilled in me. My grandfather Asael died in East Stockholm, St. Lawrence County, New York, after having received the Book of Mormon, and read it nearly through; and he declared that I was the very prophet that he had long known would come in his family. (*D.H.C.* II, 443)

True and False Prophets

My enemies say that I *have* been a true prophet. Why, I had rather be a fallen true prophet than a false prophet. When a man goes about prophesying, and commands men to obey his teachings, he must either be a true or false prophet. False prophets always arise to oppose the true prophets and they will prophesy so very near the truth that they will deceive almost the very chosen ones. (*D.H.C.* VI, 364)

Prophecy by Joseph Smith, August 6, 1842

Passed over the river to Montrose, Iowa, in company with General Adams, Colonel Brewer, and others, and witnessed the installation of the officers of the Rising Sun Lodge Ancient York Masons, at Montrose, by General James Adams, Deputy Grand-Master of Illinois. While the Deputy Grand-Master was engaged in giving the requisite instructions to the Master-elect, I had a conversation with a number of brethren in the shade of the building on the subject of our persecutions in Missouri and the constant annoyance which has followed us since we were driven from that state. I prophesied that the Saints would continue to suffer much affliction and would be driven to the Rocky Mountains, many would apostatize, others would be put to death by our persecutors or lose their lives in consequence of exposure or disease, and some of you will live to go and assist in making settlements and build cities and see the Saints become a mighty people in the midst of the Rocky Mountains. (*D.H.C.* V, 85)

Statement of Anson Call Regarding Rocky Mountain Prophecy

. . . With quite a number of his brethren, he (Joseph Smith) crossed the Mississippi River to the town of Montrose, to be present at the installment of the Masonic Lodge of the "Rising Sun." A block schoolhouse had been prepared with shade in front, under which was a barrel of ice water. Judge George (James) Adams was the highest authority in the state of Illinois, and had been sent there to organize this lodge. . . . Joseph, as he was tasting the cold water, warned the brethren not to be too free with it. With the tumbler still in his hand he prophesied that the Saints would yet go to the Rocky Mountains; and, said he, this water tastes much like that of the crystal streams that are running from the snow-capped mountains. We will let Mr. Call describe this prophetic scene: "I had before seen him in a vision and now saw while he was talking his countenance change to white; not the deadly white of a bloodless face, but a living brilliant white. He seemed absorbed in gazing at something at a great distance, and said, 'I am gazing upon the valleys of those mountains.' This was followed by a vivid description of the scenery of these mountains, as I have since become acquainted with it. Pointing to Shadrach Roundy and others, he said: 'There are some men here who shall do a great work in that land.' Pointing to me, he said: 'There is Anson, he shall go and shall assist in building up cities from one end of the country to the other, and you, rather extending the idea to all those he had spoken of, shall perform as great a work as has been done by man, so that

the nations of the earth shall be astonished, and many
of them will be gathered in that land and assist in building
cities and temples, and Israel shall be made to rejoice.'

"It is impossible to represent in words this scene which
is still vivid in my mind, of the grandeur of Joseph's appearance, his beautiful descriptions of this land, and his wonderful prophetic utterances as they emanated from the
glorious inspirations that overshadowed him. There was
a force and power in his exclamations of which the following is but a faint echo: 'Oh, the beauty of those snow-
capped mountains! The cool refreshing streams that are
running down through those mountain gorges!' Then
gazing in another direction, as if there was a change of
locality: 'Oh, the scenes that this people will pass through!
The dead that will lie between here and there.' Then
turning in another direction as if the scene had again
changed: 'Oh, the apostasy that will take place before
my brethren reach the land! But,' he continued, 'the
priesthood shall prevail over its enemies, triumph over the
devil and be established upon the earth, never more to
be thrown down!' He then charged us with the great force
and power, to be faithful to those things that had been
and should be committed to our charge, with the promise
of all the blessings that the priesthood could bestow.
'Remember these things and treasure them up. Amen.' "
(*Tullidge's Histories,* Vol. II. History of Northern Utah,
and Southern Idaho.—Biographical Supplement, p. 271
et seq. as quoted in *D.H.C.* V, 85-86)

Prophecy

. . . I gave some important instructions, and prophesied
that within five years we should be out of the power of
our old enemies, whether they were apostates or of the
world; and told the brethren to record it, that when it
comes to pass they need not say they had forgotten the
saying. (*D.H.C.* VI, 225)

Stephen A. Douglas Prophecy

Judge, you will aspire to the presidency of the United States; and if ever you turn your hand against me or the Latter-day Saints, you will feel the weight of the hand of Almighty upon you; and you will live to see and know that I have testified the truth to you; for the conversation of this day will stick to you through life.

He (Judge Douglas) appeared very friendly, and acknowledged the truth and propriety of President Smith's remarks. (*D.H.C.* V, 394)

Prophecy regarding the Westward Movement of the Saints

I instructed the Twelve Apostles to send out a delegation and investigate the locations of California and Oregon, and hunt out a good location, where we can remove to after the temple is completed, and where we can build a city in a day, and have a government of our own, get up into the mountains, where the devil cannot dig us out, and live in a healthful climate, where we can live as old as we have a mind to. (*D.H.C.* VI, 222)

A Prophecy regarding His Death

. . . *"I am going like a lamb to the slaughter, but I am calm as a summer's morning. I have a conscience void of offense toward God and toward all men. If they take my life I shall die an innocent man, and my blood shall cry from the ground for vengeance, and it shall be said of me 'He was murdered in cold blood!'"* (*D.H.C.* VI, 555)

A Prophecy

I told Stephen Markham that if I and Hyrum were ever taken again we should be massacred, or I was not a prophet of God. I want Hyrum to live to avenge my blood, but he is determined not to leave me. (*D.H.C.* VI, 546)

A Prophecy

Several of the officers of the troops in Carthage, and other gentlemen, curious to see the Prophet, visited Joseph in his room. General Smith asked them if there was anything in his appearance that indicated he was the desperate character his enemies represented him to be; and he asked them to give him their honest opinion on the subject. The reply was, "No, sir, your appearance would indicate the very contrary, General Smith; but we cannot see what is in your heart, neither can we tell what are your intentions." To which Joseph replied, "Very true, gentlemen, you cannot see what is in my heart, and you are therefore unable to judge me or my intentions; but I can see what is in your hearts, and will tell you what I see. I can see that you thirst for blood and nothing but my blood will satisfy you. It is not for crime of any description that I and my brethren are thus continually persecuted and harassed by our enemies, but there are other motives and some of them I have expressed, so far as relates to myself; and inasmuch as you and the people thirst for blood, I prophesy, in the name of the Lord, that you shall witness scenes of blood and sorrow to your entire satisfaction. Your souls shall be perfectly satiated with blood, and many of you who are now present shall have an opportunity to face the cannon's mouth from sources you think not of; and those people that desire this great evil upon me and my brethren, shall be filled with regret and sorrow because of the scenes of desolation and distress that await them. They shall seek for peace, and shall not be able to find it. Gentlemen, you will find what I have told you to be true." (*D.H.C.* VI, 566)

The Greatness and Mission of John the Baptist

The question arose from the saying of Jesus—"Among those that are born of women there is not a greater prophet than John the Baptist; but he that is least in the kingdom of God is greater than he." How is it that John was considered one of the greatest of prophets? His miracles could not have constituted his greatness.

First. He was entrusted with a divine mission of preparing the way before the face of the Lord. Whoever had such a trust committed to him before or since? No man.

Secondly. He was entrusted with the important mission, and it was required at his hands, to baptize the Son of Man. Whoever had the honor of doing that? Whoever had so great a privilege and glory? Whoever led the Son of God into the waters of baptism, and had the privilege of beholding the Holy Ghost descend in the form of a dove, or rather in the *sign* of the dove, in witness of that administration? The sign of the dove was instituted before the creation of the world, a witness for the Holy Ghost, and the devil cannot come in the sign of a dove. The Holy Ghost is a personage, and is in the form of a personage. It does not confine itself to the *form* of the dove, but in *sign* of the dove. The Holy Ghost cannot be transformed into a dove; but the sign of a dove was given to John to signify the truth of the deed, as the dove is an emblem or token of truth and innocence.

Thirdly. John, at that time, was the only legal administrator in the affairs of the kingdom there was then on the earth, and holding the keys of power. The Jews had to obey his instructions or be damned, by their own law; and Christ himself fulfilled all righteousness in becoming obedient to the law which he had given to Moses on the mount, and thereby magnified it and made it honorable, instead of destroying it. The son of Zacharias wrested the keys, the kingdom, the power, the glory from the Jews, by the holy anointing and decree of heaven, and these three reasons constitute him the greatest prophet born of woman.

Second question: How was the least in the kingdom of heaven greater than he?

In reply I asked—Whom did Jesus have reference to as being the least? Jesus was looked upon as having the least claim in God's kingdom, and [seemingly] was least entitled to their credulity as a prophet; as though he had said—"He that is considered the least among you is greater than John—that is I myself." (*D.H.C.* V, 260-261)

CHAPTER SIXTEEN

Admonition and Advice

A Man of God

A man of God should be endowed with wisdom, knowledge, and understanding, in order to teach and lead the people of God. (*D.H.C.* V, 426)

The Value of Aged Men in Counsel

The way to get along in any important matter is to gather unto yourselves wise men, experienced and aged men, to assist in council in all times of trouble. Handsome men are not apt to be wise and strong-minded men; but the strength of a strong-minded man will generally create coarse features, like the rough, strong bough of the oak. You will always discover in the first glance of a man, in the outlines of his features something of his mind. (*D.H.C.* V, 389)

Greater Faith Needed in Our Day

Darkness prevails at this time as it did at the time Jesus Christ was about to be crucified. The powers of darkness strove to obscure the glorious Sun of righteousness, that began to dawn upon the world, and was soon to burst in great blessings upon the heads of the faithful; and let me tell you, brethren, that great blessings await us at this time, and will soon be poured out upon us, if we are faithful in all things, for we are even entitled to greater spiritual blessings than they were, because they had Christ in person with them, to instruct them in the great plan of salvation. His personal presence we have

not, therefore we have need of greater faith, on account
of our peculiar circumstances; and I am determined to do
all that I can to uphold you, although I may do many
things inadvertently that are not right in the sight of God.
(*D.H.C.* II, 308)

Don't Make Hasty Moves—Be Cautious

I advise all of you to be careful what you do, or you
may by-and-by find out that you have been deceived.
Stay yourselves; do not give way; don't make any hasty
moves, you may be saved. If a spirit of bitterness is in
you, don't be in haste. You may say, that man is a sinner.
Well, if he repents, he shall be forgiven. Be cautious:
await. When you find a spirit that wants bloodshed,—
murder, the same is not of God, but is of the devil. Out
of the abundance of the heart of man the mouth speaketh.
(*D.H.C.* VI, 315)

Live by Every Word of God

Dear Brother:—In answer to yours of May 4th,
concerning the Latter-day Saints' forming a temperance
society, we would say, as Paul said—"Be not unequally
yoked . . . with unbelievers, but contend for the faith once
delivered to the Saints"; (II Cor. 6:14) and as Peter ad-
vises, so say we, "Add to your knowledge, temperance."
(II Pet. 1:6) As Paul said he had to become all things
to all men, that he might thereby save some, so must the
elders of the last days do; and, being sent out to preach
the Gospel and warn the world of the judgments to come,
we are sure, when they teach as directed by the Spirit,
according to the revelations of Jesus Christ, that they will
preach the truth and prosper without complaint. Thus
we have no new commandment to give, but admonish
elders and members to live by every word that proceedeth
forth from the mouth of God, lest they come short of the
glory that is reserved for the faithful. (*D.H.C.* V, 404)

Agents Unto Ourselves

. . . Search the scriptures—search the revelations which we publish, and ask your Heavenly Father, in the name of his Son Jesus Christ, to manifest the truth unto you, and if you do it with an eye single to his glory nothing doubting, he will answer you by the power of his Holy Spirit. You will then know for yourselves and not for another. You will not then be dependent on man for the knowledge of God; nor will there be any room for speculation. No; for when men receive their instruction from him that made them, they know how he will save them. Then again we say: Search the scriptures, search the prophets, and learn what portion of them belongs to you and the people of the nineteenth century. You, no doubt, will agree with us, and say, that you have no right to claim the promises of the inhabitants before the flood; that you cannot found your hopes of salvation upon the obedience of the children of Israel when journeying in the wilderness, nor can you expect that the blessings which the apostles pronounced upon the churches of Christ eighteen hundred years ago were intended for you. Again, if others' blessings are not your blessings, others' curses are not your curses; you stand then in these last days, as all have stood before you, agents unto yourselves, to be judged according to your works. (*D.H.C.* I, 282)

Observe Gospel Principles

Brethren, from henceforth, let truth and righteousness prevail and abound in you; and in all things be temperate; abstain from drunkenness, and from swearing, and from all profane language, and from everything which is unrighteous or unholy; also from enmity, and hatred, and covetousness, and from every unholy desire. Be honest one with another, for it seems that some have come short of these things, and some have been uncharitable, and have manifested greediness. . . . Zion shall yet live, though she seem to be dead.

Remember that whatsoever measure you mete out to others, it shall be measured to you again. (*D.H.C.* III, 233)

Beware of Pride

. . . beware of pride also; for well and truly hath the wise man said, that pride goeth before destruction, and a haughty spirit before a fall. And again, outward appearance is not always a criterion by which to judge our fellow man; but the lips betray the haughty and overbearing imaginations of the heart; by his words and his deeds let him be judged. Flattery also is a deadly poison. A frank and open rebuke provoketh a good man to emulation; and in the hour of trouble he will be your best friend. . . . (*D.H.C.* III, 295)

Humility and Simplicity Advised

How vain and trifling have been our spirits, our conferences, our councils, our meetings, our private as well as public conversations—too low, too mean, too vulgar, too condescending for the dignified characters of the called and chosen of God, according to the purposes of his will, from before the foundation of the world! We are called to hold the keys of the mysteries of those things that have been kept hid from the foundation of the world until now. Some have tasted a little of these things, many of which are to be poured down from heaven upon the heads of babes; yea, upon the weak, obscure and despised ones of the earth. Therefore we beseech of you, brethren, that you bear with those who do not feel themselves more worthy than yourselves, while we exhort one another to a reformation with one and all, both old and young, teachers and taught, both high and low, rich and poor, bond and free, male and female; let honesty, and sobriety, and candor, and solemnity, and virtue, and pureness, and meekness, and simplicity crown our heads in every place; and in fine, become as little children, without malice, guile or hypocrisy. (*D.H.C.* III, 295-296)

Friendship

Pure friendship always becomes weakened the very moment you undertake to make it stronger by penal oaths and secrecy. (*D.H.C.* III, 303)

Humility

Again, let the Twelve and all Saints be willing to confess all their sins, and not keep back a part; and let the Twelve be humble, and not be exalted, and beware of pride, and not seek to excel one above another, but act for each other's good, and pray for one another, and honor our brother or make honorable mention of his name, and not backbite and devour our brother. (*D.H.C.* III, 383-384)

Evils of Hasty Judgment

I preached to the Saints, setting forth the evils that existed, and that would exist, by reason of hasty judgment, or decisions upon any subject given by any people, or in judging before they had heard both sides of a question. I also cautioned the Saints against men who came amongst them whining and growling about their money, because they had kept the Saints, and borne some of the burden with others, and thus thinking that others, who are still poorer, and have borne greater burdens than they themselves, ought to make up their losses. I cautioned the Saints to beware of such, for they were throwing out insinuations here and there, to level a dart at the best interests of the Church, and if possible destroy the character of its Presidency. (*D.H.C.* III, 27)

Responsibility of Latter-day Saints

. . . let every one labor to prepare himself for the vineyard, sparing a little time to comfort the mourners;

to bind up the brokenhearted; to reclaim the backslider; to bring back the wanderer; to re-invite into the kingdom such as have been cut off, by encouraging them to lay to while the day lasts, and work righteousness, and with one heart and one mind, prepare to help redeem Zion, that goodly land of promise, where the willing and the obedient shall be blessed. Souls are as precious in the sight of God as they ever were; and the elders were never called to drive any down to hell, but to persuade and invite all men everywhere to repent, that they may become the heirs of salvation. It is the acceptable year of the Lord: liberate the captives that they may sing hosanna. The priests, too, should not be idle: their duties are plain, and unless they do them diligently, they cannot expect to be approved. Righteousness must be the aim of the Saints in all things, and when the covenants are published, they will learn that great things must be expected from them. Do good and work righteousness with an eye single to the glory of God, and you shall reap your reward when the Lord recompenses every one according to his work. The teachers and deacons are the standing ministers of the Church and in the absence of other officers, great things and holy walk are required of them. They must strengthen the members' faith; persuade such as are out of the way to repent, and turn to God and live; meekly persuade and urge everyone to forgive one another all their trespasses, offenses and sins, that they may work out their own salvation with fear and trembling. Brethren, bear and forbear one with another, for so the Lord does with us. Pray for your enemies in the Church and curse not your foes without: for vengeance is mine, saith the Lord, and I will repay. To every ordained member, and to all, we say, be merciful and you shall find mercy. Seek to help save souls, not to destroy them: for verily you know, that "there is more joy in heaven, over one sinner that repents, than there is over ninety and nine just persons that need no repentance." Strive not about the mysteries of the kingdom; cast not your pearls before swine, give not the bread of the children to dogs, lest you and the children should suffer, and you thereby offend your righteous Judge. (*D.H.C.* II, 229-230)

Advice to the Brethren

We would say to the brethren, seek to know God in your closets, call upon him in the fields. Follow the directions of the Book of Mormon, and pray over, and for your families, your cattle, your flocks, your herds, your corn, and all things that you possess; ask the blessing of God upon all your labors, and everything that you engage in. Be virtuous and pure; be men of integrity and truth; keep the commandments of God; and then you will be able more perfectly to understand the difference between right and wrong—between the things of God and the things of men; and your path will be like that of the just, which shineth brighter and brighter unto the perfect day. (*D.H.C.* V, 31)

Refrain from Accusing the Brethren

. . . I charged the Saints not to follow the example of the adversary in accusing the brethren, and said, "If you do not accuse each other, God will not accuse you. If you have no accuser you will enter heaven, and if you will follow the revelations and instructions which God gives you through me, I will take you into heaven as my back load. If you will not accuse me, I will not accuse you. If you will throw a cloak of charity over my sins, I will over yours—for charity covereth a multitude of sins. What many people call sin is not sin; I do many things to break down superstition, and I will break it down; . . ." (*D.H.C.* IV, 445)

Men Should Not Aspire to Higher Offices in the Church

He spoke of the disposition of many men to consider the lower offices in the Church dishonorable, and to look with jealous eyes upon the standing of others who are called to preside over them; that it was the folly and nonsense of the human heart for a person to be aspiring to other stations than those to which they are appointed of God for them to occupy; that it was better for individuals to magnify their respective callings, and wait patiently till God shall say to them, "Come up higher." (*D.H.C.* IV, 603)

Hold the Tongue—Do Not Condemn Others

I have one request to make of the President and members of the society, that you search yourselves—the tongue is an unruly member—hold your tongues about things of no moment—a little tale will set the world on fire. At this time, the truth on the guilty should not be told openly, strange as this may seem, yet this is policy. We must use precaution in bringing sinners to justice, lest in exposing these heinous sins we draw the indignation of a Gentile world upon us (and, to their imagination, justly too). It is necessary to hold an influence in the world, and thus spare ourselves an extermination; and also accomplish our end in spreading the Gospel, or holiness, in the earth. If we were brought to desolation, the disobedient would find no help. There are some who are obedient, yet men cannot steady the ark—my arm cannot do it—God must steady it. To the iniquitous show yourselves merciful.

I am advised by some of the heads of the Church to tell the Relief Society to be virtuous, but to save the Church from desolation and the sword; beware, be still, be prudent, repent, reform, but do it in a way not to destroy all around you. I do not want to cloak iniquity— all things contrary to the will of God, should be cast from us, but don't do more hurt than good, with your tongues— be pure in heart. Jesus designs to save the people out of their sins. Said Jesus, "Ye shall do the work, which ye see me do." These are the grand keywords for the society to act upon. If I were not in your midst to aid and counsel

you, the devil would overcome you. I want the innocent
to go free—rather spare ten iniquitous among you, than
condemn one innocent one. "Fret not thyself because of
evil doers." God will see to it. (*D.H.C.* V, 20-21)

The Prophet Objected to Anyone Leaving a
Meeting Early

President Joseph Smith said: "As president of this
house, I forbid any man leaving just as we are going to
close the meeting. He is no gentleman who will do it. I
don't care who does it, even if it were the king of England.
I forbid it." (*D.H.C.* V, 363)

Objection to Leaving Meetings Early

. . . It is an insult to a meeting for persons to leave
just before its close. If they must go out, let them go half
an hour before. No gentlemen will go out of meeting just
at closing. (*D.H.C.* V, 338-339)

The Sacrament

Previous to the administration, I spoke of the propriety of this institution in the Church, and urged the
importance of doing it with acceptance before the Lord,
and asked, How long do you suppose a man may partake
of this ordinance unworthily, and the Lord not withdraw
his Spirit from him? How long will he thus trifle with
sacred things, and the Lord not give him over to the buffetings of Satan until the day of redemption? The Church
should know if they are unworthy from time to time to
partake, lest the servants of God be forbidden to administer it. Therefore our hearts ought to be humble, and
we to repent of our sins, and put away evil from among
us. (*D.H.C.* II, 204)

Promises of God Not to Be Trifled With

. . . I told them it was presumption for anyone to
provoke a serpent to bite him, but if a man of God was

accidentally bitten by a poisonous serpent, he might have
faith, or his brethren might have faith for him, so that the
Lord would hear his prayer and he might be healed; but
when a man designedly provokes a serpent to bite him, the
principle is the same as when a man drinks deadly poison
knowing it to be such. In that case no man has any claim
on the promises of God to be healed. (*D.H.C.* II, 95-96)

Illness among the Saints

. . . You that have little faith in your elders when you
are sick, get some little simple remedy in the first stages. If
you send for a doctor at all, send in the first stages.
(*D.H.C.* VI, 59)

Signs to Follow Them That Believe

President Smith continued the subject, by quoting the
commission given to the ancient apostles in Mark, 16th
chapter, 15th, 16th, 17th, 18th verses, "Go ye into all the
world, and preach the Gospel to every creature. He that
believeth and is baptized shall be saved; but he that believeth not shall be damned. And these signs shall follow
them that believe: In my name shall they cast out devils;
they shall speak with new tongues; they shall take up
serpents; and if they drink any deadly thing, it shall not
hurt them; they shall lay hands on the sick, and they shall
recover."

No matter who believeth, these signs, such as healing
the sick, casting out devils, etc., should follow all that believe, whether male or female. He asked the Society if
they could not see by this sweeping promise, that wherein
they are ordained, it is the privilege of those set apart to
administer in that authority, which is conferred on them;
and if the sisters should have faith to heal the sick, let
all hold their tongues, and let everything roll on. (*D.H.C.*
IV, 603)

Trust in God when Ill

I preached to a large congregation at the stand, on the science and practice of medicine, desiring to persuade the Saints to trust in God when sick, and not in an arm of flesh, and live by faith and not by medicine, or poison; and when they were sick, and had called for the elders to pray for them, and they were not healed, to use herbs and mild food. (*D.H.C.* IV, 414)

Simple Remedies Should Be Used in Treating Sickness

... People will seldom die of disease, provided we know it seasonably, and treat it mildly, patiently and perseveringly, and do not use harsh means.

It is like the Irishman's digging down the mountain. He does not put his shoulder to it to push it over, but puts it in his wheelbarrow, and carries it away day after day, and perseveres in it until the whole mountain is removed. So we should persevere in the use of simple remedies, and not push against the constitution of the patient, day after day; and the disease will be removed and the patient saved. It is better to save the life of a man than to raise one from the dead. (*D.H.C.* V, 366)

Word of Wisdom

President Joseph Smith, Jun., made a few remarks on the Word of Wisdom, giving the reason of its coming forth, saying it should be observed. (*D.H.C.* III, 15)

Use of Liquors Discussed

... I spoke at great length on the use of liquors, and showed that they were unnecessary, and operate as a poison in the stomach, and that roots and herbs can be found to effect all necessary purposes. (*D.H.C.* IV, 299)

Hypocrisy Condemned

I love that man better who swears a stream as long as my arm yet deals justice to his neighbors and mercifully deals his substance to the poor, than the long, smooth-faced hypocrite. (*D.H.C.* V, 401)

Evil and the Relation of Evil Does Mischief in the Church

Although I do wrong, I do not the wrongs that I am charged with doing: the wrong that I do is through the frailty of human nature, like other men. No man lives without fault. Do you think that even Jesus, if he were here, would be without fault in your eyes? His enemies said all manner of evil against him—they all watched for iniquity in him. How easy it was for Jesus to call out all the iniquity of the hearts of those whom he was among!

The servants of the Lord are required to guard against those things that are calculated to do the most evil. The little foxes spoil the vines—little evils do the most injury to the Church. If you have evil feelings, and speak of them to one another, it has a tendency to do mischief. These things result in those evils which are calculated to cut the throats of the heads of the Church.

When I do the best I can—when I am accomplishing the greatest good, then the most evils and wicked surmisings are got up against me. I would to God that you would be wise. I now counsel you, that if you know anything calculated to disturb the peace or injure the feelings of your brother or sister, hold your tongues, and the least harm will be done. (*D.H.C.* V, 140)

CHAPTER SEVENTEEN

Interesting Truths Made Known

Description of Paul the Apostle

By the Prophet Joseph, January 5, 1841. "At the organization of a school for instruction. Description of Paul: He is about five feet high; very dark hair; dark complexion; dark skin; large Roman nose; sharp face; small, black eyes, penetrating as eternity; round shoulders, a whining voice, except when elevated, and then it almost resembled the roaring of a lion. He was a good orator, active and diligent, always employing himself in doing good to his fellow man." (Franklin D. Richards and Elder James A. Little, *A Compendium of the Doctrines of the Gospel,* 1925 Edition, p. 270)

Mahonri Moriancumer, the Brother of Jared

While residing in Kirtland, Elder Reynolds Cahoon had a son born to him. One day when President Joseph Smith was passing his door he called the Prophet in and asked him to bless and name the baby. Joseph did so and gave the boy the name of Mahonri Moriancumer. When he had finished the blessing he laid the child on the bed, and turning to Elder Cahoon he said, "The name I have given your son is the name of the brother of Jared; the Lord has just shown [or revealed] it to me." Elder William F. Cahoon, who was standing near heard the Prophet make this statement to his father; and this was the first time the name of the brother of Jared was known in the Church in this dispensation. (George Reynolds, "The Jaredites," *The Juvenile Instructor,* Volume 27, p. 282. Also: *Improvement Era,* Volume VIII, p. 705)

John the Revelator among the Ten Tribes of Israel

In addition to the spiritual manifestations already mentioned as having occurred at this conference of June 3rd-6th, it should be said that, according to John Whitmer's History of the Church (ch. v), "The Spirit of the Lord fell upon Joseph in an unusual manner, and he prophesied that John the Revelator was then among the Ten Tribes of Israel who had been led away by Salmanasser, king of Assyria, to prepare them for their return from their long dispersion, to again possess the land of their fathers. He prophesied many more things that I have not written." (*D.H.C.* I, 176)

The Language of Adam

In the evening a few of the brethren came in, and we conversed upon the things of the kingdom. He [Joseph Smith] called upon me [Brigham Young] to pray; in my prayer I spoke in tongues. As soon as we arose from our knees, the brethren flocked around him, and asked his opinion concerning the gift of tongues that was upon me. He told them it was the pure Adamic language. Some said to him they expected he would condemn the gift Brother Brigham had, but he said, "No, it is of God." (*Millennial Star*, XXV, 439. Also *D.H.C.* I, 297 footnote)

This Earth Formed Out of Other Planets

"The world and earth are not synonymous terms. The world is the human family.—This earth was organized or formed out of other planets which were broken up and remodeled and made into one on which we live. The elements are eternal. . . . In the translation 'without form and void, it should read, empty and desolate. The word created should be formed or organized.'" (Franklin D. Richards and Elder James A. Little, *A Compendium of the Doctrines of the Gospel*, 1925 Edition, 271)

Vision of the Celestial Kingdom

The heavens were opened upon us, and I beheld the celestial kingdom of God, and the glory thereof, whether in the body or out I cannot tell. I saw the transcendent beauty of the gate through which the heirs of that kingdom will enter, which was like unto circling flames of fire; also the blazing throne of God, whereon were seated the Father and the Son. I saw the beautiful streets of that kingdom, which had the appearance of being paved with gold. I saw Fathers Adam and Abraham, and my father and mother, my brother, Alvin, that has long since slept, and marveled how it was that he had departed this life before the Lord had set his hand to gather Israel the second time, and had not been baptized for the remission of sins.

Thus came the voice of the Lord unto me, saying—

REVELATION

All who have died without a knowledge of this Gospel, who would have received it if they had been permitted to tarry, shall be heirs of the celestial kingdom of God; also all that shall die henceforth without a knowledge of it, who would have received it with all their hearts, shall be heirs of that kingdom, for I, the Lord, will judge all men according to their works, according to the desire of their hearts.

And I also beheld that all children who die before they arrive at the years of accountability, are saved in the celestial kingdom of heaven. I saw the Twelve Apostles of the Lamb, who are now upon the earth, who hold the keys of this last ministry, in foreign lands, standing together in a circle much fatigued, with their clothes tattered and feet swollen, with their eyes cast downward, and Jesus standing in their midst, and they did not behold him. The Savior looked upon them and wept. . . . I saw Elder Brigham Young standing in a strange land, in the far south and west, in a desert place, upon a rock in the midst of about a dozen men of color, who appeared hostile. He was preaching to them in their own tongue, and the angel of God standing above his head, with a drawn sword in his hand, protecting him, but he did not see it. And I finally saw the Twelve in the celestial kingdom of God. (*D.H.C.* II, 380-381)

Zelph, the Lamanite

On the top of the mound were stones which presented the appearance of three altars having been erected one above the other, according to the ancient order; and the remains of bones were strewn over the surface of the ground. The brethren procured a shovel and a hoe, and removing the earth to the depth of about one foot, discovered the skeleton of a man, almost entire, and between his ribs the stone point of a Lamanitish arrow, which evidently produced his death. Elder Burr Riggs retained the arrow. The contemplation of the scenery around us produced peculiar sensations in our bosoms; and subsequently the visions of the past being opened to my understanding by the Spirit of the Almighty, I discovered that the person whose skeleton we had seen was a white Lamanite, a large, thick-set man, and a man of God. His name was Zelph. He was a warrior and chieftain under the great prophet Onandagus, who was known from the eastern sea to the Rocky mountains. The curse was taken from Zelph, or, at least, in part—one of his thigh bones was broken by a stone flung from a sling, while in battle, years before his death. He was killed in battle by the arrow found among his ribs, during a great struggle with the Lamanites. (*D.H.C.* II, 79-80)

Lehi's Travels

Lehi's Travels.—Revelation to Joseph the Seer. The course that Lehi and his company traveled from Jerusalem to the place of their destination:

They traveled nearly a south, southeast direction until they came to the nineteenth degree of north latitude; then, nearly east to the Sea of Arabia, then sailed in a southeast direction, and landed on the continent of South America, in Chile, thirty degrees south latitude. (Franklin D. Richards and Elder James A. Little, *A Compendium of the Doctrines of the Gospel,* 1925 edition, p. 272)

Architecture

In the afternoon, Elder William Weeks (whom I had employed as architect of the temple,) came in for instruction. I instructed him in relation to the circular windows designed to light the offices in the dead work of the arch between stories. He said that round windows in the broad side of a building were a violation of all the known rules of architecture, and contended that they should be semicircular—that the building was too low for round windows. I told him I would have the circles, if he had to make the temple ten feet higher than it was originally calculated; that one light at the centre of each circular window would be sufficient to light the whole room; that when the whole building was thus illuminated, the effect would be remarkably grand. "I wish you to carry out *my* designs. I have seen in vision the splendid appearance of that building illuminated, and will have it built to the pattern shown me." (*D.H.C.* VI, 196-197)

A Nephite Altar or Tower at Adam-ondi-Ahman

. . . We pursued our course up the river, [Grand] mostly through timber, for about eighteen miles, when we arrived at Colonel Lyman Wight's home. He lives at the foot of Tower Hill (a name I gave the place in consequence of the remains of an old Nephite altar or tower that stood there), where we camped for the Sabbath.

In the afternoon I went up the river about half a mile to Wight's Ferry, accompanied by President Rigdon, and my clerk, George W. Robinson, for the purpose of selecting and laying claim to a city plat near said ferry in Daviess County, township 60, ranges 27 and 28, and sections 25, 36, 31, and 30, which the brethren called "Spring Hill," but by the mouth of the Lord it was named Adam-ondi-Ahman, because, said he, it is the place where Adam shall come to visit his people, or the Ancient of Days shall sit, as spoken of by Daniel the Prophet. (*D.H.C.* III, 34-35)

Death of the Savior

[April 6, 1833] . . . The day was spent in a very agreeable manner, in giving and receiving knowledge which appertained to this last kingdom—it being just 1800 years since the Savior had laid down his life that men might have everlasting life, and only three years since the Church had come out of the wilderness, preparatory for the last dispensation. (*D.H.C.* I, 337)

Haste Needed in the Work of This Dispensation

. . . By and by I saw the Prophet again, [after Joseph Smith's death] and I got the privilege to ask him a question. "Now," said I, "I want to know why you are in a hurry. I have been in a hurry all through my life but I expected my hurry would be over when I got into the kingdom of heaven, if I ever did." Joseph said, "I will tell you, Brother [Wilford] Woodruff, every dispensation that has had the priesthood on the earth and has gone into the celestial kingdom, has had a certain amount of work to do to prepare to go to the earth with the Savior when he goes to reign on the earth. Each dispensation has had ample time to do this work. We have not. We are the last dispensation, and so much work has to be done and we need to be in a hurry in order to accomplish it." (*The Deseret News Weekly*, Vol. 53, No. 21, November 7, 1896)

The Name "Nauvoo"

The name of our city (Nauvoo) is of Hebrew origin, and signifies a beautiful situation, or place, carrying with it, also, the idea of rest; and is truly descriptive of the most delightful location. (*D.H.C.* IV, 268)

What Paul and the Prophet Joseph Smith Saw

Paul saw the third heavens, and I more. (*D.H.C.* V, 392)

The Lost Manuscript of the Book of Mormon

. . . I would inform you that I translated by the gift and power of God, and caused to be written, one hundred and sixteen pages, the which I took from the Book of Lehi, which was an account abridged from the plates of Lehi, by the hand of Mormon; . . . (*D.H.C.* I, 56)

CHAPTER EIGHTEEN

Statements Regarding the Scriptures

Value of the Doctrine and Covenants

My time was occupied closely in reviewing the commandments and sitting in conference, for nearly two weeks, for from the first to the twelfth of November (1831) we held four special conferences. In the last which was held at Brother Johnson's, in Hiram, after deliberate consideration, in consequence of the book of revelations, now to be printed, being the foundation of the Church in these last days, and a benefit to the world, showing that the keys of the mysteries of the kingdom of our Savior are again entrusted to man; and the riches of eternity within the compass of those who are willing to live by every word that proceedeth out of the mouth of God—therefore the conference voted that they prize the revelations to be worth to the Church the riches of the whole earth, speaking temporally. The great benefits to the world which result from the Book of Mormon and the revelations, which the Lord has seen fit in his infinite wisdom to grant unto us for our salvation, and for the salvation of all that will believe, were duly appreciated; . . . (*D.H.C.* I, 235-236)

What the Book of Mormon Is

The Book of Mormon is a record of the forefathers of our western tribes of Indians; having been found through the ministration of an holy angel, and translated into our own language by the gift and power of God, after having been hid up in the earth for the last fourteen hundred years, containing the word of God which was delivered unto them. By it we learn that our western tribes of Indians are descendants from that Joseph who was sold into Egypt, and that the land of America is a promised land unto them, and unto it all the tribes of Israel will come, with as many of the Gentiles as shall comply with the requisitions of the new covenant. (*D.H.C.* I, 315)

The Book of Mormon

. . . I told the brethren that the Book of Mormon was the most correct of any book on earth, and the keystone of our religion, and a man would get nearer to God by abiding by its precepts, than by any other book. (*D.H.C.* IV, 461)

Definition of the Word "Mormon" and the Language of the Book of Mormon

The error I speak of is the definition of the word *Mormon*. It has been stated that this word was derived from the Greek word *mormo*. This is not the case. There was no Greek or Latin upon the plates from which I, through the grace of the Lord, translated the Book of Mormon. Let the language of the book speak for itself.

On the 523rd page of the fourth edition, it reads: "And now, behold we have written this record according to our knowledge in the characters which are called among us the Reformed Egyptian, being handed down and altered by us, according to our manner of speech; and if our plates had been sufficiently large, we should have written in Hebrew; but the Hebrew hath been altered by us also; and if we could have written in Hebrew, behold, ye would have had no imperfection in our record. But the Lord knoweth the things which we have written, and also that none other people knoweth our language; therefore he hath prepared means for the interpretation thereof."

Here, then, the subject is put to silence; for "none other people knoweth our language"; therefore the Lord, and not man, had to interpret, after the people were all dead. And, as Paul said, "The world by wisdom know not God"; so the world by speculation are destitute of revelation; and as God in his superior wisdom has always given his Saints, wherever he had any on the earth, the same spirit, and that spirit, as John says, is the true spirit of prophecy, which is the testimony of Jesus. I may safely say that the word *Mormon* stands independent of the wisdom and learning of this generation. . . .

The word *Mormon*, means literally, more good. (*D.H.C.* V, 399-400)

Errors in the Bible

I believe the Bible as it read when it came from the pen of the original writers. Ignorant translators, careless transcribers, or designing and corrupt priests have committed many errors. As it read, Gen. 6:6, "It repented the Lord that he had made man on the earth"; also, Num. 23:19, "God is not a man, that he should lie; neither the Son of man, that he should repent"; which I do not believe. But it ought to read, "It repented *Noah* that God made man." This I believe, and then the other quotation stands fair. If any man will prove to me, by one passage of Holy Writ, one item I believe to be false, I will renounce and disclaim it as far as I promulgated it.

The first principles of the Gospel, as I believe, are, faith, repentance, baptism for the remission of sins, with the promise of the Holy Ghost.

Look at Heb. 6:1 for contradictions—"Therefore leaving the principles of the doctrine of Christ, let us go on unto perfection." If a man leaves the principles of the doctrine of Christ, how can he be saved in the principles? This is a contradiction. I don't believe it. I will render it as it should be—"Therefore *not* leaving the principles of the doctrine of Christ, let us go on unto perfection, not laying again the foundation of repentance from dead works, and of faith toward God, of the doctrine of baptisms, and of laying on of hands, and of resurrection of the dead, and of eternal judgment." (*D.H.C.* VI, 57-58)

The Figures Used in the Book of Revelation

It is not very essential for the elders to have knowledge in relation to the meaning of beasts, and heads and horns, and other figures made use of in the revelations; still, it may be necessary, to prevent contention and division and do away with suspense. If we get puffed up by thinking that we have much knowledge, we are apt to get a contentious spirit, and correct knowledge is necessary to cast out that spirit.

The evil of being puffed up with correct (though useless) knowledge is not so great as the evil of contention. Knowledge does away with darkness, suspense and doubt; for these cannot exist where knowledge is. (*D.H.C.* V, 340)

The Beasts and the Four and Twenty Elders Mentioned in Revelation 5:8

. . . The subject particularly referred to was the four beasts and four-and-twenty elders mentioned in Revelation—"And when he had taken the book, the four beasts and four and twenty elders fell down before the Lamb, having every one of them harps, and golden vials full of odours, which are the prayers of saints." (Rev. 5:8)

Father Brown has been to work and confounded all Christendom by making out that the four beasts represented the different kingdoms of God on the earth. The wise men of the day could not do anything with him, and why should we find fault? Anything to whip sectarianism, to put down priestcraft, and bring the human family to a knowledge of the truth. A club is better than no weapon for a poor man to fight with.

Father Brown did whip sectarianism, and so far so good; but I could not help laughing at the idea of God

making use of the figure of a *beast* to represent his kingdom
on the earth, consisting of men, when he could as well
have used a far more noble and consistent figure. What!
the Lord make use of the figure of a creature of the brute
creation to represent that which is much more noble,
glorious, and important—the glories and majesty of his
kingdom? By taking a lesser figure to represent a greater,
you missed it that time, old gentleman; but the sectarians
did not know enough to detect you.

When God made use of the figure of a beast in visions
to the prophets he did it to represent those kingdoms which
had degenerated and become corrupt, savage and beast-
like in their dispositions, even the degenerate kingdoms
of the wicked world; but he never made use of the figure
of a beast nor any of the brute kind to represent his
kingdom.

Daniel says (ch. 7, v. 16) when he saw the vision of
the four beasts, "I came near unto one of them that stood
by, and asked him the truth of all this"; the angel in-
terpreted the vision to Daniel; but we find, by the interpretation that the figures of beasts had no allusion to the
kingdom of God. You there see that the beasts are spoken
of to represent the kingdoms of the world, the inhabitants
whereof were beastly and abominable characters; they
were murderers, corrupt, carnivorous, and brutal in their
dispositions. The lion, the bear, the leopard, and the ten-
horned beast represented the kingdoms of the world, says
Daniel; for I refer to the prophets to qualify my observations which I make, so that the young elders who know
so much, may not rise up like a flock of hornets and sting
me. I want to keep out of such a wasp-nest.

There is a grand difference and distinction between
the visions and figures spoken of by the ancient prophets,
and those spoken of in the revelations of John. The things
which John saw had no allusion to the scenes of the days
of Adam, Enoch, Abraham, or Jesus, only so far as is plainly
represented by John, and clearly set forth by him. John

saw that only which was lying in futurity and which was shortly to come to pass. See Rev. 1:1-3, which is a key to the whole subject: "The Revelation of Jesus Christ, which God gave unto him, to shew unto his servants things which must shortly come to pass; and he sent and signified it by his angel unto his servant John: Who bare record of the word of God, and of the testimony of Jesus Christ, and of all things that he saw. Blessed is he that readeth, and they that hear the words of this prophecy, and keep those things that are written therein: for the time is at hand." Also Rev. 4:1. "After this I looked, and, behold, a door was opened in heaven: and the first voice which I heard was as it were of a trumpet talking with me; which said, Come up hither, and I will show thee things which must be hereafter."

The four beasts and twenty-four elders were out of every nation; for they sang a new song, saying, "Thou art worthy to take the book, and to open the seal thereof: for thou wast slain, and hast redeemed us to God by thy blood out of every kindred, and tongue, and people, and nation;" (Rev. 5:9) It would be great stuffing to crowd all nations into four beasts and twenty-four elders.

Now, I make this declaration, that those things which John saw in heaven had no allusion to anything that had been on the earth previous to that time, because they were the representation of "things which must shortly come to pass," and not of what has already transpired. John saw beasts that had to do with things on the earth, but not in past ages. The beasts which John saw had to devour the inhabitants of the earth in days to come. "And I saw when the Lamb opened one of the seals, and I heard, as it were the noise of thunder, one of the four beasts saying, Come and see. And I saw, and beheld a white horse: and he that sat on him had a bow; and a crown was given unto him: and he went forth conquering, and to conquer. And when he had opened the second seal, I heard the second beast say, Come and see. And there went out another

horse that was red: and power was given to him that sat
thereon to take peace from the earth, and that they should
kill one another: and there was given unto him a great
sword." (Rev. 6:1-4) The Book of Revelation is one of
the plainest books God ever caused to be written.

The revelations do not give us to understand anything
of the past in relation to the kingdom of God. What John
saw and speaks of were things which he saw in heaven;
those which Daniel saw were on and pertaining to the
earth.

I am now going to take exceptions to the present
translation of the Bible in relation to these matters. Our
latitude and longitude can be determined in the original
Hebrew with far greater accuracy than in the English
version. There is a grand distinction between the actual
meaning of the prophets and the present translation. The
prophets do not declare that they saw a beast or beasts,
but that they saw the *image* or *figure* of a beast. Daniel
did not see an actual bear or a lion, but the images or
figures of those beasts. The translation should have been
rendered "image" instead of "beast," in every instance
where beasts are mentioned by the prophets. But John saw
the actual beast in heaven, showing to John that beasts
did actually exist there, and not to represent figures of
things on the earth. When the prophets speak of seeing
beasts in their visions, they mean that they saw the images,
they being types to represent certain things. At the same
time they received the interpretation as to what those
images or types were designed to represent.

I make this broad declaration, that whenever God
gives a vision of an image, or beast, or figure of any kind,
he always holds himself responsible to give a revelation
or interpretation of the meaning thereof, otherwise we are
not responsible or accountable for our belief in it. Don't
be afraid of being damned for not knowing the meaning
of a vision or figure, if God has not given a revelation
or interpretation of the subject.

John saw curious looking beasts in heaven; he saw every creature that was in heaven—all the beasts, fowls and fish in heaven,—actually there, giving glory to God. How do you prove it? "And every creature which is in heaven, and on the earth, and under the earth, and such as are in the sea, and all that are in them, heard I saying, Blessing, and honour, and glory, and power, be unto him that sitteth upon the throne, and unto the Lamb for ever and ever." (Rev. 5:13)

I suppose John saw beings there of a thousand forms, that had been saved from ten thousand times ten thousand earths like this—strange beasts of which we have no conception: all might be seen in heaven. The grand secret was to show John what there was in heaven. John learned that God glorified himself by saving all that his hands had made, whether beasts, fowls, fishes or men; and he will glorify himself with them.

Says one, "I cannot believe in the salvation of beasts." Any man who would tell you that this could not be, would tell you that the revelations are not true. John heard the words of the beasts giving glory to God, and understood them. God who made the beasts could understand every language spoken by them. The four beasts were four of the most noble animals that had filled the measure of their creation, and had been saved from other worlds, because they were perfect: they were like angels in their sphere. We are not told where they came from, and I do not know; but they were seen and heard by John praising and glorifying God.

The popular religionists of the day tell us, forsooth, that the beasts spoken of in Revelation represent kingdoms. Very well, on the same principle we can say that the twenty-four elders spoken of represent beasts; for they are all spoken of at the same time, and are represented as all uniting in the same acts of praise and devotion.

This learned interpretation is all as flat as a pancake! "What do you use such vulgar expressions for, being a

prophet?" Because the old women understand it—they
make pancakes. Deacon Homespun said the earth was flat
as a pancake, and ridiculed the science which proved to
the contrary. The whole argument is flat, and I don't
know of anything better to represent it. The world is full
of technicalities and misrepresentation, which I calculate
to overthrow, and speak of things as they actually exist.

Again, there is no revelation to prove that things do
not exist in heaven as I have set forth, nor yet to show that
the beasts meant anything but beasts; and we never can
comprehend the things of God and of heaven, but by revelation. We may spiritualize and express opinions to all
eternity; but that is no authority. (*D.H.C.* V, 340-344)

A Discussion of Revelations 13:1-8

He then read Rev. 13:1-8. John says, "And I saw one
of his heads as it were wounded to death; and his deadly
wound was healed; and all the world wondered after the
beast." Some spiritualizers say the beast that received the
wound was Nebuchadnezzar, some Constantine, some Mo-
hammed, and others the Roman Catholic Church; but we
will look at what John saw in relation to this beast. Now
for the wasp's nest. The translators have used the term
"dragon" for devil. Now it was a beast that John saw in
heaven, and he was then speaking of "things which must
shortly come to pass"; and consequently the beast that
John saw could not be Nebuchadnezzar. The beast John
saw was an actual beast, and an actual intelligent being
gives him his power, and his seat, and great authority. It
was not to represent a beast in heaven: it was an angel
in heaven who has power in the last days to do a work.

"All the world wondered after the beast," Nebuchadnezzar and Constantine the Great not excepted. And if the
beast was all the world, how could the world wonder after
the beast? It must have been a wonderful beast to cause
all human beings to wonder after it; and I will venture to
say that when God allows the old devil to give power to

the beast to destroy the inhabitants of the earth, all will wonder. Verse 4 reads, "And they worshipped the dragon which gave power unto the beast: and they worshipped the beast, saying, Who is like unto the beast? Who is able to make war with him?"

Some say it means the kingdom of the world. One thing is sure, it does not mean the kingdom of the Saints. Suppose we admit that it means the kingdoms of the world, what propriety would there be in saying, Who is able to make war with my great big self? If these spiritualized interpretations are true, the book contradicts itself in almost every verse. But they are not true.

There is a mistranslation of the word *dragon* in the second verse. The original word signifies the devil, and not dragon, as translated. In chapter 12, verse 9, it reads, "That old serpent called the devil," and it ought to be translated *devil* in this case and not dragon. It is some-times translated Apollyon. Everything that we have not a keyword to, we will take it as it reads. The beasts which John saw and spoke of as being in heaven, were actually living in heaven, and were actually to have power given to them over the inhabitants of the earth, precisely according to the plain reading of the revelations. I give this as a key to the elders of Israel. The independent beast is a beast that dwells in heaven, abstract [apart] from the human family. The beast that rose up out of the sea should be translated the image of a beast, as I have referred to it in Daniel's vision. (*D.H.C.* V, 344-345)

The Parables of Jesus and the Interpretation of the Scriptures

In reference to the prodigal son, I said it was a subject I had never dwelt upon; that it was understood by many to be one of the intricate subjects of the scriptures; and even the elders of this Church have preached largely upon it, without having any rule of interpretation. What is the rule of interpretation? Just no interpretation at all. Understand it precisely as it reads. I have a key by which I understand the scriptures. I enquire, what was the question which drew out the answer, or caused Jesus to utter the parable? It is not national; it does not refer to Abraham, Israel or the Gentiles, in a national capacity, as some suppose. To ascertain its meanings, we must dig up the root and ascertain what it was that drew the saying out of Jesus.

While Jesus was teaching the people, all the publicans and sinners drew near to hear him; "and the Pharisees and scribes murmured, saying, This man receiveth sinners, and eateth with them." This is the keyword which unlocks the parable of the prodigal son. It was given to answer the murmurings and questions of the Sadducees and Pharisees, who were querying, finding fault, and saying, "How is it that this man, as great as he pretends to be, eats with publicans and sinners?" Jesus was not put to it so, but he could have found something to illustrate his subject, if he had designed it for a nation or nations; but he did not. It was for men in an individual capacity; and all straining on this point is a bubble. "This man receiveth sinners and eateth with them." And he spake this parable unto them—"What man of you, having an hundred sheep, if he lose one of them, doth not leave the ninety-and-nine in the wilderness, and go after that which is lost, until he find it? And when he hath found it, he layeth it on his shoulders, rejoicing. And when he cometh home, he calleth together his friends and neighbors, saying unto them, Rejoice with me; for I have found my sheep which was lost. I say unto you, that likewise joy shall be in heaven over one sinner that repenteth, more than over ninety-and-nine just persons which need no repentance." (See Luke 15:4-7) The hundred sheep represent one hundred Sadducees and Pharisees, as though Jesus had said, "If you Sadducees and Pharisees are in the sheepfold, I have no mission for you; I am sent to look up sheep that are lost; and when I have found them, I will back them up and make joy in heaven."

This represents hunting after a few individuals, or one poor publican, which the Pharisees and Sadducees despised.

He also gave them the parable of the woman and her ten pieces of silver, and how she lost one, and searching diligently, found it again, which gave more joy among the friends and neighbors than the nine which were not lost; like I say unto you, there is joy in the presence of the angels of God over one sinner that repenteth, more than over ninety-and-nine just persons that are so righteous; they will be damned anyhow; you cannot save them. (*D. H. C.* V, 261-262)

Peter's Writings

. . . Peter penned the most sublime language of any of the apostles. (*D.H.C.* V, 392)

Chapter Nineteen

Answers to Questions and Maxims of the Prophet

Answers to Questions Frequently Asked of the Prophet

First—"Do you believe the Bible?"

If we do, we are the only people under heaven that does, for there are none of the religious sects of the day that do.

Second—"Wherein do you differ from other sects?"

In that we believe the Bible, and all other sects profess to believe their interpretations of the Bible, and their creeds.

Third—"Will everybody be damned, but Mormons?"

Yes, and a great portion of them, unless they repent, and work righteousness.

Fourth—"How and where did you obtain the Book of Mormon?"

Moroni, who deposited the plates in a hill in Manchester, Ontario county, New York, being dead and raised again therefrom, appeared unto me, and told me where they were, and gave me directions how to obtain them. I obtained them, and the Urim and Thummim with them, by the means of which I translated the plates; and thus came the Book of Mormon.

Fifth—"Do you believe Joseph Smith, Jun., to be a prophet?"

Yes, and every other man who has the testimony of Jesus. For the testimony of Jesus is the spirit of prophecy. (Rev. 19:10)

Sixth—"Do the Mormons believe in having all things in common?"

No.

Seventh—"Do the Mormons believe in having more wives than one?"

No, not at the same time. But they believe that if their companion dies, they have a right to marry again. But we do disapprove of the custom, which has gained in the world, and has been practiced among us, to our great mortification, in marrying in five or six weeks, or even in two or three months, after the death of their companion. We believe that due respect ought to be had to the memory of the dead, and the feelings of both friends and children.

Eighth—"Can they [the Mormons] raise the dead?"

No, nor can any other people that now lives, or ever did live. But God can raise the dead, through man as an instrument.

Ninth—"What signs does Joseph Smith give of his divine mission?"

The signs which God is pleased to let him give, according as his wisdom thinks best, in order that he may judge the world agreeably to his own plan.

Tenth—"Was not Joseph Smith a money digger?"

Yes, but it was never a very profitable job for him, as he only got fourteen dollars a month for it.

Eleventh—"Did not Joseph Smith steal his wife?"

Ask her, she was of age, she can answer for herself.

Twelfth—"Do the people have to give up their money when they join his Church?"

No other requirement than to bear their proportion of the expenses of the Church, and support the poor.

Thirteenth—"Are the Mormons abolitionists?"

No, unless delivering the people from priestcraft, and the priests from the power of Satan, should be considered abolition. But we do not believe in setting the Negroes free.

Fourteenth—"Do they not stir up the Indians to war, and to commit depredations?"

No, and they who reported the story knew it was false when they put it in circulation. These and similar reports are palmed upon the people by the priests, and this is the only reason why we ever thought of answering them.

Fifteenth—"Do the Mormons baptize in the name of 'Joe' Smith?"

No, but if they did, it would be as valid as the baptism administered by the sectarian priests.

Sixteenth—"If the Mormon doctrine is true, what has become of all those who died since the days of the apostles?"

All those who have not had an opportunity of hearing the Gospel, and being administered unto by an inspired man in the flesh, must have it hereafter, before they can be finally judged.

Seventeenth—"Does not 'Joe' Smith profess to be Jesus Christ?"

No, but he professes to be his brother, as all other Saints have done and now do: Matt. 12:49-50, "And he stretched forth his hand toward his disciples and said, Behold my mother and my brethren! For whosoever shall do the will of my Father, which is in heaven, the same is my brother, and sister, and mother."

Eighteenth—"Is there anything in the Bible which licenses you to believe in revelation nowadays?"

Is there anything that does not authorize us to believe so? If there is, we have, as yet, not been able to find it.

Nineteenth—"Is not the canon of the scriptures full?"

If it is, there is a great defect in the book, or else it would have said so.

Twentieth—"What are the fundamental principles of your religion?"

The fundamental principles of our religion are the testimony of the apostles and prophets, concerning Jesus Christ, that he died, was buried, and rose again the third day, and ascended into heaven; and all other things which pertain to our religion are only appendages to it. But in connection with these, we believe in the gift of the Holy Ghost, the power of faith, the enjoyment of the spiritual gifts according to the will of God, the restoration of the house of Israel, and the final triumph of truth. (*D.H.C.* III, 28-30)

Maxims of Joseph Smith

The man who willeth to do well, we should extol his virtues, and speak not of his faults behind his back.

A man who wilfully turneth away from his friend without a cause, is not easily forgiven.

The kindness of a man should never be forgotten.

That person who never forsaketh his trust, should ever have the highest place of regard in our hearts, and our love should never fail, but increase more and more, and this is my disposition and these my sentiments. (*D.H.C.* I, 444)

. . . A good man will speak good things and holy principles, and an evil man evil things. . . .

You cannot go anywhere but where God can find you out. (*D.H.C.* VI, 366)

The Savior has the words of eternal life. Nothing else can profit us.

There is no salvation in believing an evil report against our neighbor.

I advise all to go on to perfection, and search deeper and deeper into the mysteries of Godliness.

A man can do nothing for himself unless God direct him in the right way; and the priesthood is for that purpose. (*D.H.C.* VI, 363)

The Prophet's Rule

. . . I made this my rule: *When the Lord commands, do it.* (*D.H.C.* II, 170)

Happiness

Happiness is the object and design of our existence; and will be the end thereof, if we pursue the path that leads to it; and this path is virtue, uprightness, faithfulness, holiness, and keeping all the commandments of God. (*D.H.C.* V, 134-135)

Singing

President Joseph Smith called upon the choir to sing a hymn and remarked that "tenor charms the ear, bass, the heart." (*D.H.C.* V, 339)

CHAPTER TWENTY

Political Government

The Constitution of the United States

. . . the Constitution of the United States is a glorious standard; it is founded in the wisdom of God. It is a heavenly banner; it is to all those who are privileged with the sweets of its liberty, like the cooling shades and refreshing waters of a great rock in a thirsty and weary land. It is like a great tree under whose branches men from every clime can be shielded from the burning rays of the sun. (*D.H.C.* III, 304)

The Constitution of the United States

. . . I am the greatest advocate of the Constitution of the United States there is on the earth. In my feelings I am always ready to die for the protection of the weak and oppressed in their just rights. The only fault I find with the Constitution is, it is not broad enough to cover the whole ground.

Although it provides that all men shall enjoy religious freedom, yet it does not provide the manner by which that freedom can be preserved, nor for the punishment of Government officers who refuse to protect the people in their religious rights, or punish those mobs, states, or communities who interfere with the rights of the people on account of their religion. Its sentiments are good, but it provides no means of enforcing them. It has but this one fault. Under its provision, a man or a people who are able to protect themselves can get along well enough; but those who have the misfortune to be weak or unpopular are left to the merciless rage of popular fury.

The Constitution should contain a provision that every officer of the Government who should neglect or refuse to extend the protection guaranteed in the Constitution should be subject to capital punishment; and then the president of the United States would not say, "*Your cause is just, but I can do nothing for you*," a governor issue exterminating orders, or judges say, "The men ought to have the protection of law, but it won't please the mob; the men must die, anyhow, to satisfy the clamor of the rabble; they must be hung, or Missouri be damned to all eternity." Executive writs could be issued when they ought to be, and not be made instruments of cruelty to oppress the innocent, and persecute men whose religion is unpopular. (*D.H.C.* VI, 56-57)

Political Motto of the Church

The Political Motto of the Church of Latter-day Saints

The Constitution of our country formed by the Fathers of liberty. Peace and good order in society. Love to God, and good will to man. All good and wholesome laws, virtue and truth above all things, and aristarchy, live for ever! But woe to tyrants, mobs, aristocracy, anarchy, and toryism, and all those who invent or seek out unrighteous and vexatious law suits, under the pretext and color of law, or office, either religious or political. Exalt the standard of Democracy! Down with that of priestcraft, and let all the people say Amen! that the blood of our fathers may not cry from the ground against us. Sacred is the memory of that blood which bought for us our liberty. (*D.H.C.* III, 9)

Nauvoo City Charter

The City Charter of Nauvoo is of my own plan and device. I concocted it for the salvation of the Church, and on principles so broad, that every honest man might dwell secure under its protective influence without distinction of sect or party. (*D.H.C.* IV, 249)

CHAPTER TWENTY-ONE

Church Government

Stakes to Be Organized

I have received instructions from the Lord that from henceforth wherever the elders of Israel shall build up churches and branches unto the Lord throughout the States, there shall be a stake of Zion. In the great cities, as Boston, New York, etc., there shall be stakes. It is a glorious proclamation, and I reserved it to the last, and designed it to be understood that this work shall commence after the washings, anointings and endowments have been performed here. (*D.H.C.* VI, 319)

Additional Stakes Needed

. . . it was necessary that there be more stakes of Zion appointed in order that the poor might have a place to gather to, "wherefore it was moved, seconded and voted unanimously that President Joseph Smith, Jun., and Sidney Rigdon be requested by this conference to go and appoint other stakes, or places of gathering, and that they receive a certificate of their appointment, signed by the clerk of the Church." (*D.H.C.* II, 514)

Offices in the Priesthood

A high priest is a member of the same Melchizedek Priesthood with the Presidency, but not of the same power or authority in the Church. The seventies are also members of the same priesthood, (i.e. the High Priesthood), are a sort of traveling council or priesthood, and may preside over a church or churches, until a high priest can be had. The seventies are to be taken from the quorum of elders, and are not to be high priests. They are subject to the direction and dictation of the Twelve, who have the keys of the ministry. All are to preach the Gospel, by the power and influence of the Holy Ghost; and no man can preach the Gospel without the Holy Ghost.

The bishop is a high priest, and necessarily so, because he is to preside over that particular branch of Church affairs, that is denominated the Lesser Priesthood, and because we have no direct lineal descendant of Aaron, to whom it would of right belong. This is the same, or a branch of the same, priesthood, which may be illustrated by the figure of the human body, which has different members, which have different offices to perform; all are necessary in their place, and the body is not complete without all the members.

From a retrospect of the requirements of the servants of God to preach the Gospel, we find few qualified even to be priests, and if a priest understands his duty, his calling, and ministry, and preaches by the Holy Ghost, his enjoyment is as great as if he were one of the presidency; and his services are necessary in the body, as are also those of teachers and deacons. Therefore, in viewing the Church as a whole, we may strictly denominate it one priesthood. (*D.H.C.* II, 477-478)

Additional Seventies to Be Called When Needed

If the first Seventy are all employed, and there is a call for more laborers, it will be the duty of the seven presidents of the first Seventy to call and ordain other seventy and send them forth to labor in the vineyard, until, if needs be, they set apart seven times seventy, and even until there are one hundred and forty-four thousand thus set apart for the ministry. . . .

Voted, that when another seventy is required, the presidency of the first Seventy shall choose, ordain, and set them apart, from among the most experienced of the elders of the Church. (*D.H.C.* II, 221-222)

The Work of the Seventies

The seventies are to constitute traveling quorums, to go into all the earth, whithersoever the Twelve Apostles shall call them. (*D.H.C.* II, 202)

Duties of the Seventies

. . . I say that the duties of the seventies are more particularly to preach the Gospel, and build up churches, rather than regulate them, that a high priest may take charge of them. If a high priest should be remiss in his duty, and should lead, or suffer the church to be led astray, depart from the ordinances of the Lord, then it is the duty of one of the seventies, acting under the special direction of the Twelve, being duly commissioned by them with their delegated authority, to go to the church, and if agreeable to a majority of the members of said church, to proceed to regulate and put in order the same; otherwise, he can have no authority to act. (*D.H.C.* IV, 129)

High Priests and Elders

The duty of a high priest is to administer in spiritual and holy things, and to hold communion with God; but not to exercise monarchial government, or to appoint meetings for the elders without their consent. And again, it is the high priests' duty to be better qualified to teach principles and doctrines, than the elders; for the office of elder is an appendage to the High Priesthood, and it concentrates and centers in one. And again, the process of laboring with members: We are to deal with them precisely as the scriptures direct. If thy brother trespass against thee, take him between him and thee alone; and, if he make thee satisfaction, thou hast saved thy brother; and if not, proceed to take another with thee, etc., and when there is no bishop, they are to be tried by the voice of the Church; and if an elder, or a high priest be present, he is to take the lead in managing the business; but if not, such as have the highest authority should preside. (*D.H.C.* I, 338-339)

Presidents of Seventies Not to Be High Priests

. . . It was ascertained that all but one or two of the presidents of the seventies were high priests, and when they had ordained and set apart any from the quorum of elders, into the quorum of seventies, they had conferred upon them the High Priesthood, also. This was declared to be wrong, and not according to the order of heaven. New presidents of the seventies were accordingly ordained to fill the places of such of them as were high priests, and the *ex officio* presidents, and such of the seventies as had been legally ordained to be high priests, were directed to unite with the high priests quorum. (*D.H.C.* II, 476)

Presidency, Apostles, and Seventies Sustained

I then made a short address, and called upon the several quorums, and all the congregation of Saints, to acknowledge the Presidency as prophets and seers, and uphold them by their prayers. They all covenanted to do so, by rising.

I then called upon the quorums and congregation of Saints to acknowledge the Twelve Apostles, who were present, as prophets, seers, revelators, and special witnesses to all the nations of the earth, holding the keys of the kingdom, to unlock it, or cause it to be done, among them, and uphold them by their prayers, which they assented to by rising.

I next called upon the quorums and congregation of Saints to acknowledge the presidents of seventies, who act as their representatives, as apostles and special witnesses to the nations, to assist the Twelve in opening the Gospel kingdom among all people, and to uphold them by their prayers, which they did by rising. (*D.H.C.* II, 417-418)

A Presiding Elder Is to Be Honored in His Position

It is not necessary that Jedediah and Joshua Grant should be ordained high priests in order to preside. They are too young. They have got into Zebedee Coltrin's habit of clipping half their words, and I intend to break them of it. If a high priest comes along, and goes to snub either of them in their presidency, because they are seventies, let them knock the man's teeth down his throat—I mean spiritually. (*D.H.C.* V, 368)

An Evangelist

An evangelist is a patriarch, even the oldest man of the blood of Joseph or of the seed of Abraham. Wherever the Church of Christ is established in the earth, there should be a patriarch for the benefit of the posterity of the Saints, as it was with Jacob in giving his patriarchal blessing unto his sons, etc. (*D.H.C.* III, 381)

Caution to Be Exercised in Ordinations

On the subject of ordination, a few words are necessary. In many instances there has been too much haste in this thing and the admonition of Paul has been too slightingly passed over, which says, "Lay hands suddenly upon no man." Some have been ordained to the ministry, and have never acted in that capacity, or magnified their calling at all. Such may expect to lose their appointment, except they awake and magnify their office. Let the elders abroad be exceedingly careful upon this subject, and when they ordain a man to the holy ministry, let him be a faithful man, who is able to teach others also; that the cause of Christ suffer not. It is not the multitude of preachers that is to bring about the glorious millennium! but it is those who are "called, and chosen, and faithful." (*D.H.C.* I, 468)

Presiding Officers Must Be Sustained by the Members

No official member of the Church has authority to go into any branch thereof, and ordain any minister for that church, unless it is by the voice of that branch. No elder has authority to go into any branch of the Church and appoint meetings, or attempt to regulate the affairs of the Church, without the advice and consent of the presiding elder of that branch. (*D.H.C.* II, 220-221)

Importance of Record Keeping Is Stressed by the Prophet

. . . It is a fact, if I now had in my possession every decision which had been had upon important items of doctrine and duties since the commencement of this work, I would not part with them for any sum of money; but we have neglected to take minutes of such things, thinking perhaps, that they would never benefit us afterwards; which, if we had them now, would decide almost every point of doctrine which might be agitated. But this has been neglected, and now we cannot bear record to the Church and to the world, of the great and glorious manifestations which have been made to us with that degree of power and authority we otherwise could, if we now had these things to publish abroad. . . . If you assemble from time to time, and proceed to discuss important questions, and pass decisions upon the same, and fail to note them down, by and by you will be driven to straits from which you will not be able to extricate yourselves, because you may be in a situation not to bring your faith to bear with sufficient perfection or power to obtain the desired information; or, perhaps, for neglecting to write these things when God had revealed them, not esteeming them of sufficient worth, the Spirit may withdraw, and God may be angry; and there is, or was, a vast knowledge, of infinite importance, which is now lost. . . .

Here let me prophesy. The time will come, when, if you neglect to do this thing, you will fall by the hands of unrighteous men. Were you to be brought before the authorities, and be accused of any crime or misdemeanor, and be as innocent as the angels of God, unless you can prove yourselves to have been somewhere else, your enemies will prevail against you; but if you can bring twelve men to testify that you were in a certain place, at that time, you will escape their hands. Now, if you will be careful to keep minutes of these things, as I have said, it will be one of the most important records ever seen; for all such decisions will ever after remain as items of doctrine and covenants. (From minutes of Instruction to the Council of the Twelve, Feb. 27, 1835. *D.H.C.* II, 198-199)

A Forerunner to the Law of Tithing

On the evening of the 29th of November, I united in prayer with Brother Oliver for the continuance of blessings. After giving thanks for the relief which the Lord had lately sent us by opening the hearts of the brethren from the east, to loan us $430; after commencing and rejoicing before the Lord on this occasion, we agreed to enter into the following covenant with the Lord, viz:

That if the Lord will prosper us in our business and open the way before us that we may obtain means to pay our debts, that we be not troubled nor brought into disrepute before the world, nor his people; after that, of all that he shall give unto us, we will give a tenth to be bestowed upon the poor in his Church, or as he shall command; and that we will be faithful over that which he has entrusted to our care, that we may obtain much; and that our children after us shall remember to observe this sacred and holy covenant; and that our children, and our children's children, may know of the same, we have subscribed our names with our own hands. (March 29, 1834. *D.H.C.* II, 174-175)

(Signed) JOSEPH SMITH, JUN.,
OLIVER COWDERY.

Law of Consecration

EXTRACT FROM THE MINUTES OF THE IOWA HIGH COUNCIL

President Joseph Smith, Jun., addressed the council on various subjects, and in particular the consecration law; stating that the affairs now before Congress was the only thing that ought to interest the Saints at present; and till it was ascertained how it would terminate, no person ought to be brought to account before the constituted authorities of the Church for any offense whatever; and [he] was determined that no man should be brought before the council in Nauvoo till that time, etc., etc. The law of consecration could not be kept here, and that it was the will of the Lord that we should desist from trying to keep it; and if persisted in, it would produce a perfect defeat of its object, and that he assumed the whole responsibility of not keeping it until proposed by himself. . . .

That this council will coincide with President Joseph Smith, Jun.'s decision concerning the consecration law, on the principle of its being the will of the Lord, and of President Smith's taking the responsibility on himself. (*D.H.C. IV*, 93-94)

Consecration of Property

Brother Edward Partridge:

Sir:—I proceed to answer your questions, concerning the consecration of property:—First, it is not right to condescend to very great particulars in taking inventories. The fact is this, a man is bound by the law of the Church, to consecrate to the Bishop, before he can be considered a legal heir to the kingdom of Zion; and this, too, without constraint; and unless he does this, he cannot be acknowledged before the Lord on the Church Book; therefore, to condescend to particulars, I will tell you that every man must be his own judge how much he should receive, and how much he should suffer to remain in the hands of the

Bishop. I speak of those who consecrate more than they need for the support of themselves and their families.

The matter of consecration must be done by the mutual consent of both parties; for to give the Bishop power to say how much every man shall have, and he be obliged to comply with the Bishop's judgment, is giving to the Bishop more power than a king has; and, upon the other hand, to let every man say how much he needs, and the Bishop be obliged to comply with his judgment, is to throw Zion into confusion, and make a slave of the Bishop. The fact is, there must be a balance or equilibrium of power, between the Bishop and the people; and thus harmony and goodwill may be preserved among you.

Therefore, those persons consecrating property to the Bishop in Zion, and then receiving an inheritance back, must reasonably show to the Bishop that they need as much as they claim. But in case the two parties cannot come to a mutual agreement, the Bishop is to have nothing to do about receiving such consecrations; and the case must be laid before a council of twelve high priests, the Bishop not being one of the council, but he is to lay the case before them. (*D.H.C.* I, 364-365)

Consecration of Property

When we consecrate our property to the Lord, it is to administer to the wants of the poor and needy, for this is the law of God; it is not for the benefit of the rich, those who have no need; . . . Now for a man to consecrate his property, wife and children, to the Lord, is nothing more nor less than to feed the hungry, clothe the naked, visit the widow and fatherless, the sick and afflicted, and do all he can to administer to their relief in their afflictions, and for him and his house to serve the Lord. In order to do this, he and all his house must be virtuous, and must shun the very appearance of evil. (*D.H.C.* III, 230-231)

Individual Ownership of Property

. . . I replied that I had a valuable farm joining the temple lot I would sell, and that there were other lands for sale in this place, and that we had no common stock business among us; that every man enjoys his own property, or can, if he is disposed, consecrate liberally or illiberally to the support of the poor and needy, or the building up of Zion. (*D.H.C.* II, 295-296)

The Prophet's Draft of Resolutions

First. Resolved—That no one be ordained to any office in the Church in this stake of Zion, at Kirtland, without the unanimous voice of the several bodies that constitute this quorum, who are appointed to do Church business in the name of said Church, viz., the Presidency of the Church; the Twelve Apostles of the Lamb; the twelve High Councilors of Kirtland; the twelve High Councilors of Zion; the Bishop of Kirtland and his counselors; the Bishop of Zion and his counselors; and the seven presidents of Seventies; until otherwise ordered by said quorums.

Second. And further resolved—That no one be ordained in the branches of said Church abroad, unless they are recommended by the voice of the respective branches of the Church to which they belong, to a general conference appointed by the heads of the Church, and from that conference receive their ordination. The foregoing resolutions were concurred in by the presidents of the Seventies.

ACTION OF THE TWELVE ON THE RESOLUTIONS GOVERNING ORDINATIONS

At one o'clock p.m. the council of the Twelve Apostles met in the house of the Lord, and after prayer and consultation upon the nature and expediency of the preceding resolutions offered in council on the 12th instant, it was unanimously agreed to offer the following amendment to the second resolution, (perfectly acquiescing in the first) viz.: That none be ordained to any office in the branches to which they belong; but to be recommended to a general conference appointed by those, or under the direction of those, who are designated in the book of Doctrine and Covenants, as having authority to ordain and set in order all the officers of the Church abroad, and from that conference receive their ordination.

THOMAS B. MARSH, Chairman
ORSON HYDE,
Wm. E. M'LELLIN, Clerks
(*D.H.C.* II, 394-395)

Order of Laying Cornerstones of Temples

If the strict order of the priesthood were carried out in the building of temples, the first stone would be laid at the southeast corner, by the First Presidency of the Church. The southwest corner should be laid next. The third, or northwest corner next; and the fourth, or northeast corner last. The First Presidency should lay the southeast cornerstone and dictate who are the proper persons to lay the other cornerstones.

If a temple is built at a distance, and the First Presidency are not present, then the Quorum of the Twelve Apostles are the persons to dictate the order for that temple; and in the absence of the Twelve Apostles, then the presidency of the stake will lay the southeast cornerstone; the Melchizedek Priesthood laying the cornerstones on the east side of the temple, and the Lesser Priesthood those on the west side. (*D.H.C.* IV, 331)

Order to Be Observed in Speaking in Councils

In the investigation of the subject [i.e. The Government of the House of the Lord], it was found that many who had deliberated upon it, were darkened in their minds, which drew forth some remarks from President Smith respecting the privileges of the authorities of the Church, that each should speak in his turn and in his place, and in his time and season, that there may be perfect order in all things; and that every man, before he makes an objection to any item that is brought before a council for consideration, should be sure that he can throw light upon the subject rather than spread darkness, and that his objection be founded in righteousness, which may be done by men applying themselves closely to study the mind and will of the Lord, whose spirit always makes manifest and demonstrates the truth to the understanding of all who are in possession of the spirit. (Jan. 15, 1836. *D.H.C.* II, 370)

Ancient Councils Compared to Councils During Joseph Smith's Time

At a council of the high priests and elders, (Orson Hyde, clerk), at my house in Kirtland, on the evening of the 12th of February (1834), I remarked that I should endeavor to set before the council the dignity of the office which had been conferred on me by the ministering of the angel of God, by his own voice, and by the voice of this Church; that I had never set before any council in all the order in which it ought to be conducted, which, perhaps, has deprived the councils of some or many blessings.

And I continued and said, no man is capable of judging a matter, in council, unless his own heart is pure; and that we frequently are so filled with prejudice, or have a beam in our own eye, that we are not capable of passing right decisions.

But to return to the subject of order; in ancient days councils were conducted with such strict propriety, that no one was allowed to whisper, be weary, leave the room, or get uneasy in the least, until the voice of the Lord, by revelation, or the voice of the council by the Spirit, was obtained, which has not been observed in this Church to the present time. It was understood in ancient days that if one man could stay in council, another could; and if the president could spend his time, the members could also; but in our councils, generally, one will be uneasy, another asleep; one praying, another not; one's mind on the business of the council, and another thinking on something else. (*D.H.C.* II, 25-26)

Instructions for High Councils

The high council met at my office, when I taught them principles relating to their duty as a council, and that they might be guided by the same in future, I ordered it to be recorded as follows: "That the council should try no case without both parties being present, or having had an opportunity to be present; neither should they hear one person's complaint before his case is brought up for trial; neither should they suffer the character of anyone to be exposed before the high council without the person being present and ready to defend him or herself; that the minds of the councilors be not prejudiced for or against any one whose case they may possibly have to act upon." (*D.H.C.* IV, 154)

Righteous Judgments by Councils

Brother Joseph then addressed the Twelve, and said that in all our councils, especially while on trial of anyone, we should see and observe all things appertaining to the subject, and discern the spirit by which either party was governed. We should be in a situation to understand every spirit and judge righteous judgment and not be asleep. We should keep order and not let the council be imposed upon by unruly conduct. The Saints need not think because I am familiar with them and am playful and cheerful, that I am ignorant of what is going on. Iniquity of any kind cannot be sustained in the Church, and it will not fare well where I am; for I am determined while I do lead the Church, to lead it right. (*D.H.C.* V, 411)

High Council Trial

The question has been asked, can a person not belonging to the Church bring a member before the high council for trial? I answer, No. (*D.H.C.* V, 336)

The Twelve and a High Council

An attempt was made in the foregoing council to criminate the Twelve before the high council for cutting off Gladden Bishop at their Bradford Conference, but their attempt totally failed. I decided that the high council had nothing to do with the Twelve, or the decisions of the Twelve. But if the Twelve erred they were accountable only to the general council of the authorities of the whole Church, according to the revelations. (*D.H.C.* II, 285)

Washing of Feet Introduced to the Twelve

... The item to which I wish the more particularly to call your attention tonight, is the ordinance of washing of feet. This we have not done as yet, but it is necessary now, as much as it was in the days of the Savior; and we must have a place prepared, that we may attend to this ordinance aside from the world.

We have not desired as much from the hand of the Lord through faith and obedience, as we ought to have done, yet we have enjoyed great blessings, and we are not so sensible of this as we should be. When or where has God suffered one of the witnesses or first elders of this Church to fall? Never, and nowhere. Amidst all the calamities and judgments that have befallen the inhabitants of the earth, his almighty arm has sustained us; men and devils have raged and spent their malice in vain. We must have all things prepared, and call our solemn assembly as the Lord has commanded us, that we may be able to accomplish his great work, and it must be done in God's own way. The house of the Lord must be prepared, and the solemn assembly called and organized in it, according to the order of the house of God; and in it we must attend to the ordinance of washing of feet. It was never intended for any but official members. It is calculated to unite our hearts, that we may be one in feeling and sentiment, and that our faith may be strong, so that Satan cannot overthrow us, nor have any power over us here. (D.H.C. II, 308-309)

Relationship of the Twelve Apostles to the Church

President Joseph Smith stated that the Twelve will have no right to go into Zion, or any of the stakes, and there undertake to regulate the affairs thereof, where there is a standing high council; but it is their duty to go abroad and regulate all matters relative to the different branches of the Church. When the Twelve are together, or a quorum of them, in any church, they will have authority to act independently, and make decisions, and those decisions will be valid. But where there is not a quorum, they will have to do business by the voice of the Church. No standing high council has authority to go into the churches abroad, and regulate the matters thereof, for this belongs to the Twelve. No standing high council will ever be established only in Zion, or one of her stakes. When the Twelve pass a decision, it is in the name of the Church, therefore it is valid. (D.H.C. II, 220)

The Calling of the Twelve Apostles Defined

President Smith proposed the following question: What importance is there attached to the calling of the Twelve Apostles, different from the other callings or officers of the Church?

After the question was discussed by Councilors Patten, Young, Smith, and M'Lellin, President Joseph Smith, Jun., gave the following decision:

They are the Twelve Apostles, who are called to the office of the Traveling High Council, who are to preside over the churches of the Saints, among the Gentiles, where there is no presidency established; and they are to travel and preach among the Gentiles, until the Lord shall command them to go to the Jews. They are to hold the keys of this ministry, to unlock the door of the kingdom of heaven unto all nations, and to preach the Gospel to every creature. This is the power, authority, and virtue of their apostleship.   OLIVER COWDERY, Clerk

(Feb. 27, 1835. *D. H. C.* II, 200)

The Twelve Apostles to Keep Together

Let the Twelve Apostles keep together. You will do more good to keep together, not travel together all the time, but meet in conference from place to place, and associate together, and not be found long apart from each other. Then travel from here to Maine, till you make a perfect highway for Saints.

It is better for you to be together; for it is difficult for a man to have strength of lungs and health to be instant in season and out of season, under all circumstances; and you can assist each other. (*D.H.C.* V, 366-367)

The Position of the Twelve

. . . the time had come when the Twelve should be called upon to stand in their place next to the First Presidency, and attend to the settling of emigrants and the business of the Church at the stakes, and assist to bear off the kingdom victoriously to the nations, and as they had been faithful, and had borne the burden in the heat of the day, that it was right that they should have an opportunity of providing something for themselves and families, and at the same time relieve him, so that he might attend to the business of translating. (*D.H.C.* IV, 403)

Authority of the Twelve

President Smith next proceeded to explain the duty of the Twelve, and their authority, which is next to the present Presidency, and that the arrangement of the assembly in this place, on the 15th instant, in placing the high councils of Kirtland next to the Presidency, was because the business to be transacted, was business relating to that body in particular, which was to fill the several quorums in Kirtland, not because they were first in office, and that the arrangements were the most judicious that could be made on the occasion; also the Twelve are not subject to any other than the First Presidency, viz., "myself," said the Prophet, "Sidney Rigdon, and Frederick G. Williams, who are now my counselors; and where I am not, there is no First Presidency over the Twelve." (*D.H.C.* II, 373-374)

The Twelve to Be Equal in Their Ministry

REVELATION TO THE TWELVE

Behold they are under condemnation, because they have not been sufficiently humble in my sight, and in consequence of their covetous desires, in that they have not dealt equally with each other in the division of the monies which came into their hands, nevertheless, some of them dealt equally, therefore they shall be rewarded; but verily I say unto you, they must all humble themselves before me, before they will be accounted worthy to receive an endowment, to go forth in my name unto all nations.

As for my servant William, let the Eleven humble themselves in prayer and in faith, and wait on me in patience, and my servant William shall return, and I will yet make him a polished shaft in my quiver, in bringing down the wickedness and abominations of men; and there shall be none mightier than he, in his day and generation, nevertheless if he repent not speedily, he shall be brought low, and shall be chastened sorely for all his iniquities he has committed against me; nevertheless the sin which he has sinned against me is not even now more grievous than the sin with which my servant David W. Patten, and my servant Orson Hyde, and my servant William E. McLellin have sinned against me, and the residue are not sufficiently humble before me.

Behold the parable which I spake concerning a man having twelve sons: for what man among you, having twelve sons, and is no respecter of them, and they serve him obediently, and he saith unto one, Be thou clothed in robes, and sit thou here; and to the other, Be thou clothed in rags, and sit thou there and looketh upon his sons, and saith, I am just? Ye will answer, and say, no man; and ye answer truly; therefore, verily thus saith the Lord your God, I appoint these Twelve that they should be equal in their ministry, and in their portion, and in their evangelical rights; wherefore they have sinned a very grievous sin, inasmuch as they have made themselves unequal, and have not hearkened unto my voice; therefore, let them repent speedily, and prepare their hearts for the solemn assembly, and for the great day which is to come, verily thus saith the Lord. Amen (*D.H.C.* II, 300-301)

Assistant Counselors to the First Presidency

MINUTES OF A CONFERENCE ASSEMBLED IN COMMITTEE OF THE WHOLE CHURCH AT KIRTLAND ON SUNDAY THE 3RD OF SEPTEMBER, 1837.

At nine o'clock in the morning George W. Robinson was called upon to take minutes of the conference. Sidney Rigdon then presented Joseph Smith, Jun., to the Church to know if they still looked upon and would still receive and uphold him as the President of the whole Church, and the vote was unanimous in the affirmative.

President Smith then presented Sidney Rigdon and Frederick G. Williams as his counselors, and to constitute with himself the three first Presidents of the Church. Voted unanimously in the affirmative, except for Frederick G. Williams, which was not carried unanimously.

President Smith then introduced Oliver Cowdery, Joseph Smith, Sen., Hyrum Smith, and John Smith for assistant counselors. These last four, together with the first three, are to be considered the heads of the Church. Carried unanimously. (*D.H.C.* II, 509)

CHAPTER TWENTY-TWO

The Articles of Faith

In March of 1842 the Prophet Joseph Smith wrote a letter to a Mr. John Wentworth, giving a brief account of the Church, its rise and progress, and a concise statement of its doctrines. These thirteen brief, pertinent statements have been adopted by the Church as "The Articles of Faith." They are basic to all of the doctrines as taught by the Prophet and for that reason are placed as the final chapter of this book. They have not been classified into the separate chapters. They were written by the Prophet at the conclusion of the letter to Mr. Wentworth, as follows:

"We believe in God the Eternal Father, and in His Son Jesus Christ, and in the Holy Ghost.

"We believe that men will be punished for their own sins, and not for Adam's transgression.

"We believe that through the Atonement of Christ all mankind may be saved by obedience to the laws and ordinances of the Gospel.

"We believe that the first principles and ordinances of the Gospel are: (1) Faith in the Lord Jesus Christ; (2) Repentance; (3) Baptism by immersion for the remission of sins; (4) Laying on of hands for the gift of the Holy Ghost.

"We believe that a man must be called of God by prophecy and by the laying on of hands, by those who are in authority, to preach the Gospel and administer in the ordinances thereof.

"We believe in the same organization that existed in the Primitive Church, viz., apostles, prophets, pastors, teachers, evangelists, etc.

"We believe in the gift of tongues, prophecy, revelation, visions, healing, interpretation of tongues, etc.

"We believe the Bible to be the word of God, as far as it is translated correctly; we also believe the Book of Mormon to be the word of God.

"We believe all that God has revealed, all that He does now reveal, and we believe that He will yet reveal many great and important things pertaining to the kingdom of God.

"We believe in the literal gathering of Israel and in the restoration of the Ten Tribes; that Zion will be built upon this [the American] continent; that Christ will reign personally upon the earth; and that the earth will be renewed and receive its paradisiacal glory.

"We claim the privilege of worshiping Almighty God according to the dictates of our own conscience, and allow all men the same privilege, let them worship how, where, or what they may.

"We believe in being subject to kings, presidents, rulers and magistrates, in obeying, honoring, and sustaining the law.

"We believe in being honest, true, chaste, benevolent, virtuous, and in doing good to *all men;* indeed we may say that we follow the admonition of Paul—We believe all things, we hope all things, we have endured many things, and hope to be able to endure all things. If there is anything virtuous, lovely, or of good report, or praiseworthy, we seek after these things." (*D.H.C.* IV, 540-541)

Index

A

Aaron, 34; priesthood of, 25

Aaronic Priesthood, 26, 27, 99

Abel, brought of the firstlings, 29

Abraham, 21, 47, 116, 154, 192; blood of, 13; literal seed of, 13; sacrifice required of, 24; ordained by Melchizedek, 25; taken to the bosom of, 59; bosom, 91; God of, 101; in the celestial kingdom, 183.

Adam, 27, 32, 58, 118, 119, 154, 192; fall of, 1; relationship to man, 2; father of the human family, 3; delivers his stewardship to Christ, 3; why he blessed his posterity, 3; retains his standing as head of the human family, 3; Son of man stands before, 3; was created in, 10; called of God to his office, 23; held the keys of the priesthood, 23; held keys first on earth, and then in heaven, 23; father of all living, 23; holds the keys, 27; who was the first man, 27; received commandments, 28; language of, 182; in the celestial kingdom, 183; transgression of, 227

Adam-ondi-Ahman, Joseph Smith saw Adam in, 3; a Nephite altar or tower at, 185

Adams, George James, 163

Adams, James, 99

Adulterous man, a sign seeker is an, 150

Adultery, 144

Advice to the brethren, 175

Agents unto ourselves, 171

Almighty, 27; inspiration of the, 9; disposed to set up stakes for the, 15; God, 228

America, 189; the whole of, is Zion, 79

American continent, 228

Anarchy, 206

Ancient councils compared to councils of Joseph Smith's time, 219

Ancient of Days, 2, 27, 94, 99, 124; shall come, 186

Angels, 103, 113, 117

Answers to questions, 200

Antediluvians, iniquities of, 1

Apollyon, 197

Apostasy, 143; sign of, 149

Apostate, respecting an, 59; God will never acknowledge any traitors or, 149

Apostles, 9, 112, 116, 154, 211, 227

Appearance of a wicked spirit, 153

Arab, send him to Arabia, 74

Arabia, Sea of, 185

Architecture, 185

Aristocracy, 206

Articles of Faith, 227

Asael Smith, 162

Assistant Counselors to the First Presidency, 225

Assyria, king of, 182

Astronomy, principles of, given to the prophet, 46

B

Baptism, 36, 102, 227; remission of sins by, 5; John's, 50; is a holy ordinance, 53; necessary for entrance into the celestial kingdom, 58; a sign ordained of God; 59; is a sign to God, 60; doctrine of, 190

Baptism for the dead, 88; doctrine of, 89; doctrine of explained, 90; justice of, 91

Baptist, 106, 157

Baptize, 35

Baptized, in the name of Jesus Christ, 5; for remission of sins, 13

Battle of Gog and Magog, 131

Baurau, meaning of, 16

Beast and the four and twenty elders, 191

Beasts in heaven, John saw curious looking, 195

Beasts which John saw, 193

Believe, liberty to think and, proposed by the Prophet, 106

Berosheit, meaning of, 16

Bible, 16, 20, 21, 79, 86, 88, 95, 119, 148, 200, 228; plurality of Gods is prominent in the, 18; errors in, 190

Bishop, 215, 216, 217; Gladden, 221

Body and spirit, difference between, 118

Boston, 208

Bow in the cloud is a sign, 122

Bow in the heavens a sign, 121

Bradford conference, 221

Bridegroom, 123